D0936938

6

THE GOLDEN THRONG

THE GOLDEN THRONG

A Book About Bees

By

EDWIN WAY TEALE

Illustrated from eighty-five
photographs by the Author

Reedsburg Public Library
345 Vine St.
Reedsburg, Wi. 53959

universe

381 PARK AVENUE SOUTH • NEW YORK, N.Y. 10016

Copyright 1940, 1968 by Edwin Way Teale
First published in U.S.A. by Dodd, Mead & Co.
First published in Britain 1942

1981 edition published by Alphabooks, Sherborne, Dorset

All rights reserved. No part of this publication
may be reproduced, stored in a retrieval system,
or transmitted, in any form or by any means,
electronic, mechanical, photocopying, recording or
otherwise, without prior permission of the
publishers.

ISBN 0 906670 20 9
Printed in Britain by Hillman Printers (Frome) Ltd, Somerset

PUBLISHER'S NOTE

The death in Autumn 1980 of Edwin Tay Teale left the world the poorer, for this American naturalist had a way of communicating his understanding of nature which is not common in the younger generation of naturalists and ecologists.

Much acclaimed as a naturalist in his own country, he reached a wide audience in the years after the war with books about travels in America, winning the Pulitzer Prize for Literature. In 1970 his book on the natural history of Britain was published, but as a young man his speciality was entomology. *The Golden Throng* was first published in England in 1942, and in spite of this unpropitious date, the book gained an immediate and enthusiastic following. Those familiar with the popular literature on the honeybee will recognize the common ground with Maeterlinck, though, of course, Teale was himself a beekeeper and his information is based on twentieth century knowledge.

Whilst his anthropomorphic approach to nature is now out of fashion, and has indeed been turned upside down by popular writers like Lorenz, Lopez and Morris, it is hard to escape its charm when applied to the bee community. We have decided, therefore, that an unedited new edition of Edwin Way Teale is the most appropriate way to make this much loved book available to modern readers, leaving the author's literary charm untouched.

Our editorial file copy is inscribed 'To Mona (Beardsley) from Michael, who loved this book.' I am quite convinced that many new readers will feel the same.

Dedicated to My Aunts

ELIZABETH WAY EDWARDS
WINNIFRED WAY WENCKE

In Memory of Days
at Lone Oak

CONTENTS

	FOREWORD	11
1	ETERNAL WAYS	17
2	RISE OF AN INSECT CITY	21
3	SPRINGTIDE	35
4	BEE'S WORLD	39
5	HONEY FLOW	49
6	TREASURE VAULTS	59
7	ENEMIES	67
8	HOUR OF THE SWARM	79
9	BIRTH OF AN INSECT QUEEN	85
10	MATING FLIGHT	91
11	NURSERIES	101
12	LAWS OF THE CITY	110
13	THE BEE IN LORE AND LEGEND	117
14	BOOKS AND BEES	131
15	WINTER	141
16	PHOTOGRAPHIC POSTSCRIPT	147
	BIBLIOGRAPHY	155
	INDEX	157

FOREWORD

THE story of the bees has been told by poets like Maeterlinck, by scientists like Huber and Lubbock, by practical beekeepers like Phillips and Root. These insects, with their harmonious, golden cities of wax, hold a perennial fascination for us. In adding this volume to the long list of bee books, I have sought—in addition to recording discoveries of recent years—to bring to the reader, through the eye of the camera, the age-old drama of life in the hive and in the bee's world of flower-filled fields. For there is beauty as well as mystery in the life of the bee. As Maeterlinck truly says, "To him who has known them and loved them, a summer where there are no bees becomes as sad and as empty as one without flowers or birds."

It is a pleasure, at this time, to set forth my indebtedness to Herbert F. Schwarz, Research Associate in *Hymenoptera* at the American Museum of Natural History, for reading the book in manuscript form and, in the light of his specialized knowledge, making invaluable suggestions. I am also indebted to him for permission to consult his manuscript translation of H. von Buttel-Reepen's *The Phylogenetic Origin of the Bee State*.

Sincere thanks are also due to Francis W. Gravely, New York manager of the A. I. Root Company, who was kind enough to check through *The Golden Throng* in manuscript form, and to Herman Harries, beekeeper of Lynbrook, L.I., without whose friendly cooperation many of the photographs reproduced in this volume would have been impossible.

EDWIN WAY TEALE

ILLUSTRATIONS

Frontispiece

BEES ON THE COMB

Between pages 32 – 33

THE GOLDEN THRONG Workers on brood comb
LONGER TONGUES Bumblebee on red clover
BUMBLEBEE ROOST Marked bumblebee on hollyhock
HAIRY BODIES Bumblebee fertilizing iris
TOO DEEP Bee on honeysuckle
POLLEN BASKETS Worker gathering pollen
BEE-GLUE HUNTER Honeybee getting propolis
WINDOWS Honeybees in an observation hive
THIRTY-SEVEN THOUSAND TRIPS AFIELD Bee on iris
TWICE ROUND THE WORLD Bees filling honeycomb
THE FACE OF A WORKER Magnified view of head
PANTRY CELLS Pollen stored near brood
PILLS OF POLLEN taken from pantry cells
SIX WEEKS IS A LIFETIME Bee on small sunflower
11,400 STROKES A MINUTE Worker on dead leaf
TRIPODS Sideview of a walking bee

Between pages 64 – 65

TEACHABLE Bee and petunia
TINY FLOWERS A worker honeybee on vetch

13

PUSSYWILLOW POLLEN   being gathered by a bee
BEAUTY   Honeybee on a rose
A MASTERPIECE OF ART AND ENGINEERING   Honeycomb
OPEN-AIR COMBS, constructed in a tree
SKEP COMB, constructed inside a straw skep
MOUNTAINS OF WAX   Bees on comb inside modern hive
SIX SIDED   Plaster cast showing hexagonal cells
FOUNDATION for honeycomb, artificially prepared
A WAX PEANUT   Queen cell taken from hive
THE FOUNDATION of a queen cell
FINISHING TOUCHES being put on queen cell
EMPTY CELL after the queen has emerged
ROYAL JELLY   Queen grub in opened cell
ROYAL NYMPH   Developing nymph of queen in cell
ROYAL BEE   The newly emerged queen
TWO ENEMIES   Dragonfly and toad
FEARSOME FOE   A praying mantis with a honeybee
THE WAX MOTH   Close-up view of insect pest
SILK-LINED TUNNELS produced by wax moth larvae
PROPOLIS   Bee-glue after use in hive
A MOUSE NEST, taken from the interior of a hive
THE QUEEN'S COURT   Queen surrounded by attendants

Between pages 96–97

THIRTY THOUSAND BEES   Picture of a swarm
SCENT SIGNALS   Close-up view of swarming bees
EGG LAYER   Queen depositing egg in cell
INVASION   Strange queen being attacked by workers
HONEYBEE EGG   Magnified picture of egg
LARVA   The grub which hatches from the egg
THIRTEEN HUNDRED MEALS A DAY   Feeding the grubs
MIRACLE   Grub beginning to turn into nymph
TRANSFORMATION   The change nearly complete

NYMPH The immature bee in later stage of development
BIRTHDAY Young bees emerging from cells
CLIMAX Close-up of emerging bee
NEWBORN View of fluffy new worker bee
LIVING FAN A worker bee fanning wings at threshold
COMMUNICATION between workers
SUICIDE OF A BEE Stinging bee pulling away abdomen
THE THRESHOLD OF THE HIVE Bees at entrance

Between pages 128 – 129

NECTAR HUNTERS among apple blossoms
THE OLD-FASHIONED STRAW SKEP
HIVING A SWARM Series showing process
MODERN HIVE with movable frames
HE HAS A GRANDFATHER BUT NO FATHER Drone's head
HOLIDAY MOOD Bees in a swarm removed with spoon
INSECT FURNACE Cluster heating hive
SUMMER SAVINGS Bees removing honey stored in comb
AUTUMN ASTERS Honeybee collecting nectar
LAST SWEETS OF AUTUMN Bees on apple
PATTERNS formed by honeycomb negatives
WINTER OVERCOATS Beehive in winter snow

1

ETERNAL WAYS

THROUGHOUT this early spring morning, the landing
stage of my observation hive has been the scene of intense
activity. Bees have crowded out of the dark interior. They have
paused, cleaned their antennae, rubbed forelegs vigorously over
their great compound eyes—as though they were sleepers awaken-
ing—and then have launched themelves into the sunny air.

Spring, sweeping northward up the globe, in recent weeks, has
set the juices of the earth flowing again. Frost-stiffness has left
the bones of the fields: the last ragged scarves of snow have disappeared from the gullies: and, everywhere, rising from the moist
soil, spreads the penetrating scent of warming earth. With their
animation, their excitement, their ceaseless comings and goings,
my bees are chronicling in action the return of warmth, of life, of
spring.

Thus, during uncounted centuries, these insects have greeted the
coming of each new summer, and, during at least forty of these
centuries, man and bees have been in partnership. Yet, even today,
these insects in many ways are an enigma to us. We often feel as
though we were standing on the fringes of the bees' world, peering
across the boundaries of that realm—so near in space, so remote
in customs and motives.

Each observer, according to the colour of his mind and the
background of his experience, sees in this insect commonwealth
individual facets of a many-sided whole. The moralist, the philosopher, the artist, the engineer, the poet, the political scientist, all

have contemplated the bees with a sense of humility and awe. Even the most unimaginative of men, if he understands the things he sees, must find in the complex civilization of the hive a source of lasting wonder.

During the earliest days of my acquaintance with the bees, I must confess there were moments of rebellion against the ordered routine of their lives. To me, the adventurous, free-lance existence of solitary insects appealed far more than the machinelike life of the social bees. The seeming sameness of the thousands of workers, the seeming infallibility of their instinctive behaviour—these were my first impressions of the golden throng.

But as I came, day after day, to know them better, to see them battling disaster which again and again threatened to engulf their city of wax, to see them meeting problems with a united front, to see marked members of the colony exhibiting individual variations of behaviour, I grew to understand the respect and affection with which millions of human beings have regarded the honeybee. I came also to understand the charm and the wonder of the bees, so often felt and remarked by the older writers.

But there is more than wonderment to be found in the commonwealth of the hive. Men today, as men of old, have discovered something calming, something reassuring in the solidarity of the swarm. It is held together by a bond that aeons and all the vicissitudes of life have failed to alter. Without benefit of pamphlets or speakers, foundations or endowments, the life of the hive forms one of the great, living philosophies of the world.

Here, cause and effect, rightness and reward, lie close to the surface and natural laws are reduced to their simplest form. In the murmurous industry of the golden throng, in the sense of order and purpose in the lives of the bees, in the certitude of their labours, the justice of their destiny, their harmony with all the forces of Nature—here, dwellers in the hives of men oftentimes have found fresh courage and a tide of returning belief in the justice of eternal ways.

They also have found a measure of peace. Like Yeats in his bee-loud glade on the Isle of Innisfree, men of many ages have discovered in the murmuring harmony of their insects healing for the mind and release from the tautness of a changing world. Most of the beekeepers I have known have found that hours spent among their hives were calming hours. The pacific, steady murmur of the well-ordered hive, like rustling leaves or lapping water, like looking at the stars or distant mountains or the sea, brings a sense of peace.

It is among the beehives of the world that we find most often a respect for, and an appreciation of, the wonders of the insect world. Here, most often, man has known a sense of comradeship with the insects, a sense of working together for understandable ends amid the mysterious forces of instinct.

This has been so for thousands of years. For the golden throng, the insects so long associated with the gold of flowers, the gold dust of pollen, the golden treasure of honey, have been familiar to man since prehistoric times. An ancient rock painting discovered in the Araña Cave, near Valencia, in Spain, depicts early tribesmen robbing the wild bees. Aboriginal peoples in many parts of the world kept these insects for the sweets they produced, and until beyond the days of the Roman Empire honey was the main sugar supply of the world. In Egypt, the honey-producing insect appears on monuments as early as 3500 B.C. Ancient records even tell us the price of strained Egyptian honey in the year 3000 B.C. It was approximately 3d. a quart.

In their long relationship with man, these ancient insects have been no servile livestock. They are no broken-spirited dependents upon human dispensation. They are self-reliant, jealous of their rights, co-operating only so long as man obeys the higher laws to which they have allegiance. Man can kill the honeybee: but he cannot conquer it. He can make it serve him only by letting it follow the dictates of its nature.

It is surprising to reflect that among the hordes of insects—those minute creatures whose varied forms outnumber a hundred times all the stars we can see with our naked eyes—that among their more than 600,000 species the honeybee should stand almost unique: virtually the only insect that can be considered as domesticated by man. The honey it produces annually is worth millions of pounds and the value of bees to orchardists, whose blooms they pollenize, is incalculable.

No one knows the precise time when these familiar insects first appeared on earth. We do know, however, that they were well established long before humankind, even in its most primitive beginnings, was known to our planet. The modern city of the hive, with its tens of thousands of inhabitants, its laws, its castes, its multitudinous and infinitely varied activity, is the product of millions of years of slow transition.

2

RISE OF AN INSECT CITY

BEFORE I take you into this teeming, close-packed city of the bees, it will help to become acquainted with some of the ancestors of the modern honey maker. Beginning with strange prehistoric insects with still stranger names, they have evolved through the ages into the familiar, efficient, present-day dweller of the hive.

As Nature has written it with fossils in amber and stone, the story of the early bees suggests some ancient and defaced volume. Only here and there you find the fragment of a page, leaving you puzzling over what came before and what followed after. Concerning the remote ancestors of the honeybee, wide chasms of the unknown separate the thin ridges of present-day knowledge.

Some time in the distant past, even before the Rockies or the Himalayas or the Alps shouldered upward on the surface of the earth, some primal ancestor of the bees, the wasps, and the ants—all members of the great *Hymenoptera* order—appeared on earth. Time passed. The great lagoons, where salt water ebbed and flowed across Kansas and the Central West, changed into marshes which in turn gave way to land that supported grass and trees and higher vegetation.

In the Mesozoic Era, roughly 100,000,000 years ago, flowering plants arrived amid the ferns and reeds of an earlier flora. It was then that the true bees, fertilizers of the blooms, appeared among the insects.

Millions of years later, in Miocene times, volcanoes ringing a prehistoric shallow sea near what is now Florissant, Colorado, exploded and blackened the sky with their dust. This fine volcanic ash drifted down on the shore of the sea. Among the thousands of insects imprisoned in its drifts were a number of prehistoric bees. That ancient tragedy has widened our knowledge of the early nectar hunters, for it has enabled scientists to study their fossil remains embedded in shale.

An even clearer window into the past are bits of amber picked up along the shores of the Baltic Sea. Made of pitch that had oozed from the great coniferous forests of prehistoric Europe, this amber sometimes contains insects in a perfect state of preservation. Within such transparent tombs, ancient bees are available for minute examination. All told, there are more than 8,500 fossil insects known to entomology. Approximately sixty have been identified as bees.

Among the more than 10,000 different species of bees living to-day, the ones most nearly forming a link with the past are *Hylaeus* and its relatives. *Hylaeus* is a primitive, almost hairless insect which is known in most sections of the United States. Usually it is black with yellow facial markings. It has only a rudimentary tongue and its hind legs are devoid of the "pollen baskets" which are so valuable to the honeybee. It swallows pollen instead of carrying it on its rear legs. *Hylaeus* lives only a single summer and stores up just enough nectar and pollen to charge a few crude cells which it hollows out within brambles or other plant stems. A curious glistening layer of material, thought to be formed of the hardened saliva of the bee, lines these cavities. After stocking the cells, *Hylaeus* deposits an egg in each. With the completion of this task, the work of the solitary insect reaches its climax. It dies in the early frosts of autumn and never sees its offspring which emerge from their bramble cradles the following summer.

Ninety-five per cent of all bees you see darting about the open fields are, like *Hylaeus*, solitary in their labours. Only about 500 of the more than 10,000 known species share the work of gathering food and caring for the young. Among these 500, however, are outstanding examples of insect co-operation, culminating in the involved organization of the hive.

In the rise of this insect city, the development is from relatively simple lives to more and more complex and co-operative units. There is, of course, no clean-cut evolutionary chain leading, link by link, from *Hylaeus* to the present-day hive dweller, *Apis mellifera*. Varied families and groups of bees, nevertheless, by their habits and life cycles, give a hint of the logical sequence of change which may have occurred in the past. Beginning with the manifold forms of those lonely labourers, the solitary bees, the record progresses through successive steps that lead to simple co-operation, elemental groupings, impermanent colonies, and, finally, the communal life of the hive—the outstanding instance of social success among the insects.

Most of the solitary bees are a step above the primitive *Hylaeus* in the climb to this long goal. These creatures often are curious insects with extraordinary habits. There is, for example, the carder bee that kindly old Gilbert White of Selborne used to watch as it filled its empty snail-shell nest with the finest ravellings of cotton and wool. There are the mason bees that cement together fragments of stone with their own saliva—bees that Jean Henri Fabre never tired of interrogating "in the language of experiment" among the stony fields of Serignan. There are the leaf cutters that, with the sharp scissors of their jaws, snip out little disks and ovals from plant leaves and flower petals. Of these they fashion the thimble-shaped cells which they stack together like paper cups to form their nests. There are a host of others: carpenter bees that bite tunnels through solid wood: cuckoo bees that surreptitiously deposit eggs in the cells of other species: the specialized *Halica-*

toides novae-angliae, which in New England are said to visit no other flowers except the purple bloom of the pickerel weed.

It is well to remember that in all of these varied habits, and in the changes that lead to increasingly complex forms of co-operation, the bee is guided largely by instinct. The short life of the individual insect permits scant time for learning. Like the chick that can stand on its feet as soon as it breaks from the shell, the honeybee is equipped with abilities and instincts that make instruction or trial-and-error learning unnecessary. It performs a sequence of actions just as a gramophone record produces a sequence of sounds, and in most cases it can no more alter the sequence than the record can continue the song after the needle passes out of the last groove. Fabre demonstrated how true this is by an ingeniously simple experiment.

Outside the hard cell of a mason bee he placed an envelope of thin paper. The emerging insect, whose jaws were capable of cutting through the rock-like wall of its prison, was baffled by the flimsy shell of the second chamber. If the paper was placed in contact with the masonry of the cell, the young bee bit its way to freedom. But if there was a space between the two, the insect, although perfectly able to escape, wandered about within its paper prison until it died. Nature had equipped it, through instinct, to bite its way out of its masonry birth chamber: but Nature had not equipped it with the ability to cope with the abnormal, once the instinctive act was finished.

On the other hand, there are many instances of bees that appear to overcome obstacles, that seem to reason out solutions to problems, that vary their instinctive behaviour slightly to meet specific needs. I have seen them produce odd-shaped cells to fill in corners and try this way and that in seeking an entrance to different flowers. Just where the dividing line between instinct and intelligence lies is difficult to decide. The question of whether bees and other insects are always ruled entirely by instinct or whether they are sometimes able to use a kind of reasoning in the solution of new problems has divided entomologists into two schools of thought. A fascinating presentation of the latter viewpoint will be found in R. W. G. Hingston's *Instinct and Intelligence.*

Even if instinct alone dictates the conduct of the insects, it provides the solitary bee with all it ever needs to know in the course of a normal existence. It passes on from generation to generation cunning and amazing stratagems for use in an endless fight for the perpetuation of the species.

One relative of the leaf cutters, *Osmia fossoria*, when it finishes making its nest and laying its eggs in an empty snail shell, is not content with blocking the entrance. It laboriously digs a hole in the ground near the shell, excavates a slanting runway up one side, rolls the shell into the hole, and covers it with dirt. Underground, the nest is safe from parasitic wasps. *Osmia bicolor*, another relative of the leaf cutters, follows a line of action even more surprising. When its eggs have been laid within the abandoned shell, it gathers a number of long pine needles. Cementing them together at the top, it forms a tepee-like shelter which hides the nest from the sight of parasitic foes.

To protect her eggs from the ovipositors of insect enemies, the mason bee, *Chalicodoma muraria*, coats the outside of her nest with armour that is almost literally as hard as iron. This coating, formed of flint-like particles cemented together with the bee's saliva, will blunt the finest steel needle. Such cells, when attached to cliffs, are so solidly cemented in place that they can be removed only with a hammer and chisel.

Among the mason bees is found a further step in the advancing record of co-operation towards the commonwealth of the social insects. Near Serignan, Fabre once calculated that the tiles of a single roof held three-quarters of a ton of material attached in the

form of nests by mason bees. Instead of seeking out solitary locations for their nest building, these insects labour close together.
In the main, each performs its individual tasks without assistance.
But all work amicably in close juxtaposition. And when the bees
have filled their cells with food and eggs and have sealed them up,
Fabre found that an interesting thing occurs. "Without drawing
distinctions between what does and what does not belong to them,"
he writes, "they set to work in common on a general protection for
the colony." Working together in co-operation for the good of all,
they produce a thick coating of mortar to cover the cells.

Here is a definite step towards the insect city. Still further progress is represented by some of the burrowing *Halictidae*. All of
these bees, which include possibly 1,000 different species, nest in
the earth or in rotten wood. Sometimes they dig their galleries as
far as six feet below the surface of the ground. Hundreds of subter-
ranean cells are constructed close together, each cell lined with
tough paper-like material. The interesting thing about the laby-
rinth of these ground bees is that, though the insects are engaged
in individual labours underground, they all make use of a common
entrance.

In 1896, a scientist in Hungary discovered that co-operation
among the *Halictidae* may go even farther. He noticed that one of
the female ground bees was blocking the entrance to the underground chambers, using her head to fill the opening. When disturbed, she would reverse her position and present her sting at the
opening of the tunnel. When one of the inmates of this insect apart-
ment house returned laden from the fields, the guard always backed
down from the doorway to let her pass. Then she quickly returned
again to her vigil at the entrance.

The scientist tried a simple experiment. With a pair of forceps,
he removed the bee guard. Another female took her place. Similarly, he removed her. A third bee barricaded the entrance. The

scientist had demonstrated that this group of supposedly solitary bees were co-operating actively for the protection of their mutual interests.

Later researches indicate that some species of these ground bees have even more in common with the fully social insects. Over-wintering females have been found to lay eggs in the spring which produce sterile "worker" insects that never mate and that spend their days caring for the brood which hatches from the eggs, laid by the *Halictidae* "queens."

This division of labour bridges the gap between the maid-of-all-work, solitary insect and the social bee. Beginning with some unknown *hymenopterous* insect—the ancient ancestor of all the bees—the record thus has progressed along a trail of increasing co-operation. From the extinct early bees of amber and stone to the primitive modern insect *Hylaeus*: from this bee of the brambles to the partial co-operation of the mason bees, and on to the *Halictidae* with their apartment-house nests with a common entrance, and finally their specialized division of labour, the record has indicated the probable steps in the advance towards the three great groups of social bees known to-day: the bumblebees, or *Bombidae*: the *Meliponidae*, or tropical stingless bees: and the *Apidae*, or hive bees.

The least complex of these three great forms of socialized insect life is the colony of the bumblebees. In temperate zones, the life of the colony begins anew each spring. Just as in the case of the solitary bees, an overwintering female begins her labours unassisted. She selects the site of the nest. She gathers the first food. She shapes the rude cell in which she lays the earliest eggs. But, unlike the solitary insect, the bumblebee queen may be surrounded, at the height of the summer season, with 300 or even 500 of her children, all labouring and co-operating for the welfare of the colony.

Usually some abandoned mouse nest, or, in the case of *Bombus affinis*, a chipmunk nest, is selected by the bumblebee queen as the home of the colony. Early in spring, she awakens from the deep sleep of her hibernation and takes wing in search of such a site. Cleaning it out, she prepares an egg cell and a thimble-like honey-pot, both made of wax. This is our first encounter with that marvellous substance. No solitary bee can create it. Only the bumblebees, the stingless bees, and the hive bees can produce it—from special glands along the segments of the abdomen.

Packing fluffy pollen into the cell she has created, the queen lays her eggs on this tiny golden mattress. From the eggs hatch grubs that consume the pollen, spin papery cocoons, and finally emerge as adult bumblebees. While this transformation has been taking place, the mother bee has been sitting on the cell in the manner of a brooding hen. So far as I know, only the earwig among all the insects sits on its eggs in a similar way.

The earliest bees born in a bumblebee colony are usually stunted. They receive less food than the later arrivals, which have the advantage of many assisting nurse bees in place of one queen. Repeatedly, I have watched bumblebees leaving and entering the door of an underground nest and have noted small bees and large bees appearing and disappearing. The small ones were not babies which had yet to reach maturity. They were the bees which hatched from the earliest eggs. In fact, the large bumblebees were the young ones and the small bumblebees the old ones!

All the arrivals at the colony during the early weeks of summer are sterile worker bees. The drones, like the young queens, are born at the climax of the colony's development, usually as autumn approaches. Unlike the egg-laying specialist, the queen of the honeybees, this queen of the bumblebee colony, in the early stages of her active adult life, engages in many tasks. She goes afield, gathers food, lays eggs, cares for the young. She possesses the all-round ability of the solitary insect whereas the *Apis mellifera* queen leads a completely specialized existence.

In fact, in the far north, where short summer seasons make the development of a regular bumblebee colony impossible, the queens are even more like solitary insects. From their eggs, it is said, no sterile workers are produced. In twenty years of collecting these insects near the Artic Circle, a Norwegian entomologist reports he caught only fertile queens, never worker bees.

At the opposite extreme from these lonely "Eskimo bees" are the bumblebees of the tropics whose colonies continue for years instead of dying out at the end of summer, as do the colonies of temperate zones. These tropical bumblebees give off swarms from time to time in the manner of the hive bee.

Towards the end of summer, temperate-zone colonies begin to break up. As early as the middle of July I have found the insects sleeping afield instead of returning to the nest. In the hollyhocks of my Long Island garden, I discovered five of these hairy, booming bees, returning night after night. By dabbing spots of quick-drying enamel on their backs one evening, I marked them with different colours. The next night, three out of the five had come home to roost in the same clump of hollyhocks and one was clinging in the identical spot where it had slept the night before.

From the last eggs laid by the bumblebee queen there develop the fertile females and the drones. These young bees mate during the waning days of summer and the new queens crawl into some retreat for the months of winter hibernation. Cold slays all the other members of the colony, leaving behind—to begin the bumble-bee cycle all over again the following spring—only the young fertilized queens. In their bodies life sinks so low during the icy months of winter that they appear hardly different from the frozen wood or earth around them. But almost as soon as the first green of reviving grass appears in the fields, they begin coursing low over meadows and weed lots, circling and zigzagging, seeking locations for their future nests.

This, then, is the way of the bumblebee, an insect that ranges from the cold southernmost tip of South America northward through temperate and torrid zones to the Arctic Circle and includes in its ranks some of the largest bees known to science. First place for size among the bees, however, goes to *Megachile pluto*, a leaf cutter from the island of Batchian. The world's tiniest bee, on the other hand, is so minute you could place eighteen, head to tail, along the back of *Megachile pluto*. This midget insect is *Trigona duckei*, a stingless bee that often alights on the hands of perspiring jungle travellers, evidently in search of moisture.

The stingless bees, in whose ranks this two-millimeter midget belongs, represent the second phase of the three types of social bee, that trio of insect societies which culminates our record of growing co-operation. Many of these insects are so small that they have been given the nickname of "mosquito bees." Another sobriquet of the tropics is "angelitos" or "little angels," a tribute to their inability to sting. In spite of the fact they are without fully developed stings, these insects have other and curious means of protecting their stores of honey. Some years ago, Dr William Morton Wheeler, of Harvard University, encountered a cloud of angry stingless bees in Central America. They landed on his face and spread over it a caustic fluid so powerful it burned away the outer layer of the skin.

Other stingless bees employ varied and cunning manœuvres to outwit their enemies. In the Malay region, for example, one species spreads a sort of tanglefoot belt around the entrance of the nest. This "unwelcome" mat traps insect intruders, such as ants, which may attempt to gain an entrance during the night. On the island of Jamaica, a black ant is the implacable enemy of a species of stingless bee which has, within its nest, honeypots as large as pigeon's eggs. To outwit these black robbers, guard bees continually barricade the entrance.

Another species of stingless bee, which lives in the interior of Australia, employs an insect version of the mediaeval rack to deal with foes that seek an entrance to the nest. As the interloper alights at the doorway, guards rush upon it, grab different legs, and pull with all their might in opposite directions. Stretched out to the limit, the captive struggles until it grows weaker and finally dies. Bees of this kind have been known to tug thus for fully an hour before they released their grip.

Within the nest of the stingless bees there is often a colony of several thousand insects. The horizontally placed comb is composed of a single layer of cells instead of two layers, back to back, as in the case with the hive bee. Among the many types of stingless bee known to science, some construct these combs in hollow trees, others in walls, others in the ground, others hanging from limbs, and still others in the nests of termites and even in those of ants. Some of the *Trigona* construct their nests without any comb structure whatever. Instead, the cells are arranged in clusters.

Unlike the bumblebees, and like the hive bees, the stingless insects of the tropics have special waxen jars for storing pollen and others for holding honey. In such colonies there are three castes, the males, the sexually undeveloped female workers, and the egg-laying queens. As in the hive, the workers make up the bulk of the population and do most of the labour connected with gathering supplies and providing for the brood.

However, in one important respect, the stingless bees fall short of the highest civilization of the honeybee. Like solitary insects, instead of feeding the larvae directly they seal over the cells after the eggs have been laid on the stored-up food. Usually, without further attention, the young hatch out, feed as larvae, change into adults, and emerge.

In other ways, the city of the honeybee—the third and final type of bee society—differs from bumblebee and stingless-bee colonies.

Here, pure wax is used in the construction of the comb. Both the bumblebee and the stingless bee produce wax. But, for many of its uses, they mix it with other materials. The honeybee, on the other hand, employs only pure wax in the construction of the light, strong framework of hexagonal cells which forms the interior of the insect city.

Life in this metropolis of wax centres in the single female capable of laying fertilized eggs—the queen. She is larger, lives longer, forms the hub about which moves the intense, ceaseless activity of the bees. In an average-sized hive there will be approximately 30,000 workers, 500 to 2,000 drones, and one queen. If a bumblebee queen dies in midsummer, the colony languishes, doomed to extinction. In the honeybee hive, however, the workers can produce a new queen if an accident befalls the old one, by feeding a larva royal jelly, the gland fluid manufactured in the heads of the worker bees.

Unlike solitary nectar feeders, and the bumblebees, the honeybee has treasure trove stored up for a time of want. This hoard of golden honey supplies the energy which enables the whole colony to endure through the months of cold—to survive when other bees have perished. This is the triumph of the hive dweller's form of life. In its organization, its discipline, its mutually helpful activity, the honeybee has found a way to persist even against tremendous odds, defeating its twin enemies, hunger and cold.

That the honeybee has maintained its way of life century after century, age after age, aeon after aeon, demonstrates how well fitted its insect commonwealth is to cope with the problems of its existence. The permanence of this city of the bees is the paramount affirmation of its harmony with natural laws.

Thus the long rise towards the complex co-operation of the beehive reaches its climax in the activity of *Apis mellifera*. The complete scientific pedigree of an individual in this golden throng reads

THE GOLDEN THRONG at work on the brood-comb within the hive. Honey-bees weigh approximately $\frac{1}{5000}$ of a pound apiece. An average colony will contain approximately 30,000 individuals and will weigh six pounds.

LONGER TONGUES permit the bumblebee to obtain nectar from red clover and other blooms which the shorter tongues of the honeybee cannot reach.

BUMBLEBEE ROOST. This photoflash picture shows a marked bumblebee which returned on successive nights to sleep in the identical hollyhock bloom.

HAIRY BODIES enable honeybees, as well as this bumblebee entering a Siberian iris, to fertilize blooms by carrying pollen from flower to flower.

TOO DEEP for the hive bee to reach is the nectar of the honeysuckle. Sometimes the insects take advantage of holes bitten near the base of the blooms by bumble-bees and thus are able to reach the desired nectar.

POLLEN BASKETS on the hind legs of this bee, working on goldenrod, enable it to transport quantities of the floral gold back to the hive in one trip.

BEE-GLUE HUNTER. From buds and plants, bees obtain the resinous propolis, or bee-glue, used for filling cracks and coating foreign objects too large for the insects to carry. Snails, and even mice, have been found within hives where they have died, coated with the sanitary bee-glue.

WINDOWS on either side of my observation hive reveal the varied, never-ending activity of the golden throng, shown here in its winter cluster.

THIRTY-SEVEN THOUSAND TRIPS AFIELD are sometimes made by bees in gathering sufficient nectar from flowers to produce one pound of honey. Members of a single colony often visit more than 250,000 blooms in the course of one day's work.

TWICE AROUND THE WORLD is the calculated mileage flown by bees in gathering enough nectar to fill comb-cells, as shown above, with one pound of honey.

THE FACE OF A WORKER honeybee. It has jaws that bite inward from the sides of the head; smelling antennae equipped with more than 2,000 sense-plates; eyes, colourblind to red, but able to see ultra-violet rays invisible to us.

PANTRY CELLS on the edge of the brood-comb hold stored-up pollen where it can be obtained quickly by nurse bees for feeding maturing grubs.

PILLS OF POLLEN, such as these, come from pantry cells near the brood-comb. Different-coloured pollen often gives them the appearance of a layer-cake.

SIX WEEKS IS A LIFETIME for the average honeybee worker at the height of the nectar-gathering season. In the open fields, more than 1,000 bees from the same colony may die in one day, exhausted by concentrated toil.

11,400 STROKES A MINUTE are made by the wings of a honeybee. When the temperature falls below 50 degrees F., the wing muscles are paralyzed. This worker, clinging to a dead leaf with the thermometer showing 48 degrees, is unable to fly but can move its legs. They become paralyzed below 45 degrees.

TRIPODS support the honeybee when it walks. The front and rear legs on one side move in unison with the middle leg on the opposite side, thus providing the insect with a firm, three-cornered support at all times.

as follows: Class, *Insecta*: Order, *Hymenoptera*: Sub-order, *Apoidea*: Family, *Apidae*: Genus, *Apis*: Species, *Mellifera*. Of this species there are, in turn, many varieties. What sort of creature is the little insect that possesses so lengthy a pedigree? The story of these nectar hunters has reached the threshold of the hive. From now on its concern will be with the inhabitants that dwell within.

3

SPRINGTIDE

A LL winter long the low murmur of the bees has filled the room in which I write. All winter they have clustered like dull golden rosettes on either side of the comb, instinctively heating the hive with the same primal muscular furnace which warmed their ancestors in hollow trees and rocky crannies before mankind was known.

Night or day, whenever I removed the wooden side of the observation hive to peer through the glass beneath, I found the cluster continually in motion at the centre, less and less active towards the fringes. It had the appearance of being formed of some heavy, yellowish fluid, viscous at the rim, bubbling in the middle. Stepping forward and backward, swaying elephant-wise from side to side, flipping their wings, moving their antennae, engaging in a sort of honeybee jig, the central insects are ceaselessly in motion. By intense muscular activity, they not only warm themselves but produce heat for the other insects of the cluster as well. Thus the whole colony is preserved through the months of cold.

Because of their small size, all insects necessarily must be cold-blooded. It is from the surface of an animal's body that most of the heat dissipates. And the smaller the creature, the greater is its surface area in proportion to its bulk. So bees, in common with other six-legged creatures, have a temperature when at rest that is approximately that of the surrounding air. The only way an insect can rise its body temperature is through chemical combustion resulting from muscular activity. The honeybee, which can neither migrate nor hibernate, makes use of this principle to maintain warmth within the hive. It alone, among all the creatures of the earth, has developed this simple and effective means of overcoming winter's cold.

As your eye travels outward from the centre of one of these clusters of close-packed bees, you notice that the insects at the rim barely move at all. How do these bees, clinging where the chill is greatest, avoid succumbing to the cold? If you continue to watch, you will shortly discover the answer.

In addition to the movement at the centre, there is a slow, continual exchange of positions between bordering bees and dancers in the central area. There is a deliberate, persistent flow from the centre to the outer edges and back again. The fringe insects change places with the bees at the centre and, in their turn beginning the furnace dance, become heated by exertion. Thus, continually shifting position, night and day, the bees alternately work and rest, heat and cool their bodies, and raise the temperature of the whole cluster to a point where life can continue.

They do not attempt to heat the whole hive—only the living clusters on the comb. In my observation hive, the two masses of bees, on either side of the comb, remain opposite each other and thus form, roughly, a ball of insects. The outer bees, with close-packed bodies, create what is in effect an insulating shell that keeps the heat within. So effective is this insulation, and the muscular furnace itself, that tests have shown the temperature within such a mass of bees to be, in times of intense cold, as much as *seventy-five degrees F.* above the thermometer reading outside the hive. In other words, it is possible for the clustering insects to enjoy a comfortable sixty-five degrees F. on nights when the mercury has fallen to ten degrees below zero.

As soon as the temperature within the hive drops to approximately fifty-seven degrees F., the insect furnace begins to function.

The bees cluster and start their dance. This mass of insects, within limits, acts as though controlled by a thermostat. The tempo of the dance speeds up or slows down, the cluster contracts or expands, as the outside temperature falls or rises.

Day after day, as winter drew on, I measured the mass on one side of the comb and noted the reading of the thermometer. At sixty degrees F., the bees spread out loosely, covering an area approximately twelve by seven inches. With the mercury standing at fifty degrees, the cluster had contracted to seven by six inches. And when the thermometer registered thirty-two degrees, the freezing point, the size of the mass was four by four and a half inches. Thus the bee cluster within the hive was responding almost like mercury to the rise and fall of the surrounding temperature.

Week after week, and month after month, this battle against cold—the common enemy of animal life—went on. Bees are scrupulously clean and on bright days, even when the thermometer stood at only a few degrees above fifty, they often left the comb for short cleansing flights in the outer air. Only drones are guilty of scattering their excrement about the hive.

Sometimes, before the bees on cleansing flights could return, they became chilled and sluggish. The wing muscles of the honeybee become inactive at temperatures below fifty degrees F., and the insect is unable to fly. Down to forty-five degrees, it is able to move its legs and walk. But when the thermometer falls below that point, the isolated, inactive bee is paralyzed by cold.

This morning, however, the terrors of winter are a thing of the past. Springtide is here. Although the colony has had causalties during the months of ice and snow, although its numbers have shrunk, sturdy survivors remain. From them will develop the thriving colony of a few weeks hence.

Already the mottled spear of the skunk cabbage has thrust its way above the marshy ground and the strange, hooded flower it bears is coming into bloom. Alder catkins and pussywillows will soon be bursting into the golden foam of pollen. The humming of my bees beyond the window, growing louder and louder, marks the beginning of that vast surge of life that runs through the wild at springtime.

The earliest treasure the bees are seeking is the gold dust of pollen. Rich in protein, it is vital to feeding those early workers of the summer colony, soon to be represented by whitish-grey elongated specks within carefully cleaned cradles of wax—the eggs of the queen bee laid in the brood cells.

But even the most meagre additions to the stores of the hive bring hope to the insects. All is no longer outgo. Soon miles on miles of blooms will lift nectar goblets for the bees to sip. Depleted stores will be replenished ; once more the colony will balance its budget with the liquid gold of honey. The insects, as well as I, sense that they have passed the icy ridges of winter and are on the border of summer's warm and fruitful valley.

Replacing the dark confinement of past months, there will be life in the open fields, life in the bee's realm of sunshine and flowers. To one of those glinting, golden specks beyond my window, how does this realm appear? How does the honeybee see and smell and feel the things around it? How do its organs function? How has Nature equipped it for the life it leads? As nearly as we can, let us imagine ourselves one of these dwellers in the city of wax, and, from its point of view, examine the world in which we live.

4

BEE'S WORLD

ONE-HALF an inch long, one-quarter of an inch high, one-five-thousandth of a pound in weight—that, in bare physical terms, describes the average honeybee.

But in that fraction of an inch between the many-lensed eyes and the pointed tip of the abdomen, the bees, now thronging into the spring sunshine beyond my observation hive, possess an amazing variety of organs. For the honeybee is a chemical factory. It is an elaborate tool kit. It is the possessor of remarkable abilities still but dimly understood. Its small size, its puny strength, are offset by many gifts of Nature.

Like all insects, the bee wears its skeleton on the outside of its body in the form of a hard, jointed suit of armour. This chitin shell takes the place of an internal structure of bones such as we possess. Also, like other insects, the bee's body is divided into three distinct zones or parts: the head—bearing the eyes, the antennae, the mouth parts, and the brain ; the thorax or middle body—to which are attached the legs and the wings ; and the abdomen—holding the reproductive organs, the heart, the digestive organs, and the sting.

Clinging to a window sill, where, a week or so ago, it died on a cleansing flight, I discover one of my bees. I place it under a magnifying glass and its dark, twin antennae, each divided into two parts by an "elbow" and each attached to the front of the head by a natural ball-and-socket joint, first come into view.

During the life of the bee, these twin feelers are constantly in use. In reality, they are smellers rather than feelers. Although other scent organs are located in various parts of the body, the antennae form the main organs of smell. They represent the noses of the bees. And throughout their lives these insects are guided largely by smell. They literally "follow their noses" to flowers; they recognize strange bees from members of their own colony by scent ; they detect stored honey by smell ; and apparently they are calmed by the odour of the queen within the hive.

Some years ago, Dr N. E. McIndoo, of the United States Department of Agriculture, reported that drones, queens, and workers all have differentiating odours. He declared that after a few months' practice he was able himself to distinguish the castes apart merely by smelling the bees. It is his theory that each individual bee within the hive has its own particular odour which can be detected by the amazingly acute smelling organs of the other inmates.

It is interesting to note that the various castes differ in the complexity of the make-up of their antennae. A queen, which rarely leaves the hive, may have only 2,000 sense plates on her two antennae. A worker bee, spending much of its time abroad in the search for nectar, may have as many as 6,000 ; while the drone, which seems to find its mate partly by scent, may have 30,000, fully five times the maximum number for the worker bee.

Behind the antennae are the great, jewel-like compound eyes, covering both sides of the head and in the drones extending almost helmetwise over the top. Each eye is composed of thousands of tiny six-sided lenses. Individual lenses record parts of the image and, in the manner of a mosaic, all of the parts fit together to form the unified visual impression which the brain receives. Between the two main organs of sight are a trio of small simple eyes. Through these five eyes, the bee sees the world around it. It is thought that the insect perceives near-by objects with the simple eyes and more distant objects with the compound ones. At any rate, moving things probably are seen more easily than stationary ones and all objects appear indistinctly and without sharpness of detail. The eye of the bee is like a fixed-focus camera ; it has no mechanism for focusing as have our eyes. Also, it has no means of closing. A bee sleeps with its eyes open.

Although bees are colour-blind in the manner of a man who sees red and green as grey, they can perceive ultra-violet rays, "black light" invisible to us. Dr Frank E. Lutz, Curator of Entomology at the American Museum of Natural History, once photographed various flowers by the ultra-violet part of sunlight which is seen by such insects. He found, among other things, that the common black-eyed Susan has a striking pattern at the tips of the petals when seen, as the bee sees it, through reflected rays of black light.

Another interesting revelation brought out by Dr Lutz's experiments concerns the familiar yellow crab spider often found hiding in flowers to prey on butterflies, bees, and other insects that alight on the petals. To our eyes, its colour provides a perfect camouflage and the theory long has been held that its yellow hue prevents its prey from seeing it until too late. However, Dr Lutz showed that the spider reflected almost none of the ultra-violet light when on some flowers, and so, to the "black-light eyes" of the bees, may stand out clearly against the flower in which it is hiding.

When first I set up my observation hive, its runway led out a window that faced west. As autumn settled down, cold winds swept day after day, out of the north-west and I shifted my hive to a room with a southern exposure. For weeks afterward, when the bees flew out on bright days, I would find scores clustering at the spot where the runway had led out the window on the other side of the house. Memory had led them to the old entrance—memory and their eyes. For the most acceptable present explanation of how bees find their way back to the hive is through eyesight, through the recognition of landmarks. Young bees always make "play flights" about the entrance, familiarizing themselves with their surroundings, before they begin longer flights afield. When such inexperienced insects are carried any distance from home, they never return; older bees, to whom the surrounding fields are familiar territory, will find their way home when released miles from the hive. The amazing beeline of the bee is a feat made possible by eyesight and memory.

At the bottom of the heart-shaped head of the bee, my magnifying glass enlarges the twin mandibles or jaws which, unlike ours, are hinged at the side and bite inward in the manner of pincers held horizontally. Queens, drones and workers all have jaws of different shapes. It is interesting to note, in passing, that those of the workers are rounded and can be used only for crushing and not for piercing or cutting. Thus these insects are physically incapable of committing an act of which they are often accused—biting through the skin of fruits to obtain the sweet juices within.

In his classic, *The Life of the Bee*, Maurice Maeterlinck aptly describes the tongue of this insect as being fashioned like some fantastic Chinese weapon. Created by centuries of evolution, it can be formed into a tube through which the bee sucks nectar from the flowers. Many tests have revealed that bees have a delicate taste sense. We know they can discover the presence of salt in such minute quantities that the human tongue cannot detect it.

But when it comes to hearing, bees are sadly lacking. It is doubtful whether they can detect sound waves at all. I have watched my bees when a cornet blast was sounded within four inches of the side of the observation hive and they showed not the slightest response. However, when, a moment later, I tapped the glass with the rubber of a pencil, the cluster of insects became excited at once. Relatively insensible to sounds, they are highly responsive to physical vibrations.

One European bird, the blue tit, uses this latter fact to the bee's disadvantage. It taps on the side of a hive. The vibrations excite the insects, and guards rush out to see what is the cause. As they appear, the tit snaps them up and, when it has made a meal, flies away.

Within the head of the bee there is a brain, but it is far different from outs. The insect brain is not the master of the whole nervous system of the body. If the head is severed, the bee still can stand upright and walk! If, on the other hand, the entire abdomen is cut away in an accident, the front part of the insect still can take food! The brain is the largest of several bundles of nerves which form the "switchboards" of the insect's nervous system and govern the operation of different parts of its body.

So much for the head of the bee. Behind the head is the "motor room" of the insect, the thorax. This hard-shelled middle body is largely filled with powerful muscles that operate the wings and legs. The thorax is concerned primarily with locomotion.

If you watch a honeybee, on some chill morning, crawling slowly along the landing stage of a hive, you will discover an interesting thing about the way it walks. It employs its six legs, three at a time, in the form of tripods. The front and rear legs on one side move in unison with the middle leg on the opposite side. Thus the insect has a three-cornered, solid support at all times.

Sharp, double-pronged claws at the bottom of each leg enable the bee to cling to flowers. In addition, its feet are equipped with sticky pads. Using them, my bees are able to walk up the smooth inside surface of the glass window of the observation hive or progress, flywise, upside down across the ceiling.

The legs of the bee, however, provide more than a means of locomotion. They form one of the most complex tool kits in all natural history. On the front legs are the antennae cleaners, through which the insects run their feelers to remove dust and dirt. On the middle legs, the workers have sharp spurs, believed to be used as pries to remove pollen from the pollen baskets on the rear legs. These latter depressions, surrounded by stiff hairs and located on the outside of the legs, permit the insects to bring home large masses of pollen. Inside the hind legs are the "pollen combs" and between two of the joints are the so-called "wax shears."

The hair, or pile, which covers the thorax of the bee is also an aid to gathering pollen. The fluffy dust catches on the hairs and is carried from flower to flower, thus fertilizing the blooms. The insect takes its share of the floral gold occasionally, combing the pollen from its furry body and packing it into the baskets of its hind legs. Frequently, a bee in flight will keep its legs busy in this process. I have sometimes seen bees hovering as they actively packed in pollen which they had collected in visiting a clump of flowers.

The amazingly efficient wings which enable the bee to navigate the air for miles and to lift loads heavier than the weight of its own body are attached to the upper part of the thorax. This keeps the centre of gravity low and increases stability in the air. Each bee has four wings, two large front ones and two small rear ones. In flight, they function as a single pair, the rear ones being attached by tiny hooks to a ridge running along the trailing edge of the front wings.

One hundred and ninety times a second, 11,400 times a minute, the honeybee beats its wings in flight. The movement, during each successive beat, is in four different directions—up, forward, down, and backward. As long ago as 1869, the French experimenter, E. J. Marey, reported that the wing of a bee, unlike the wing of the bird, describes a figure of eight in the air. Marey attached bits of gold leaf to the tips of an insect's wings and then watched the glinting pattern the blurring wings produced when the insect was held in a beam of light. Later experimenters used smoked paper, carried rapidly past insects secured so that the tips of their wings traced a pattern on the record sheet. Recently, Dr R. E. Edgerton and Dr E. A. Chadwick, of Harvard University, have turned their superspeed motion-picture camera upon insects in flight. The later tests have confirmed Marey's pioneer discovery.

No machine man has ever made approaches the honeybee as an efficient navigator of the air. The bees outside my window are hovering, climbing, darting forward, stopping abruptly, swinging sidewise, flying backward. They zoom at a steep angle up the side of the house. Later in the summer, they will return across miles of fields bearing loads of nectar equal to half their total weight. And, in autumn, my workers will give an even more amazing exhibition of their lifting capacity on the wing. They will carry away the bodies of dead drones—drones that weigh far more than they do.

In 1918, a scientific paper printed in Jena, Germany, threw light upon the manner in which bees are able to lift such tremendous loads. By suspending rows of fine owl feathers (so light they moved in the slightest breath of air) from a frame with horizontal crossbars, R. Demoll determined the direction of the air currents created by the wings of an insect secured below the frame. He found that the air was being pulled down towards the insect from the front and top of the wings. In other words, the wings of the bee act like propellers turned forward and upward, pulling the insect aloft more in the manner of a helicopter than of an aeroplane.

During flight, the motion of the wings is determined by two types of muscles, vertical and longitudinal. The vertical muscles lift the wings and the horizontal ones depress them. The shape of the thorax alters continually during flight. It is interesting to note that if you press on the thorax of a freshly killed bee you will see the wings change their position.

Have you ever watched a bee during a moment when it was at rest? If you have, you probably noticed that its abdomen seemed to lengthen and shorten slightly in fairly rapid succession. This is the breathing of the bee. The lengthening and shortening of the abdomen corresponds roughly to the rising and falling of our chests. But the bee has no lungs. Instead, it possesses a series of branching tubes which carry the air to all parts of the body from twenty openings in the sides, two pairs in the thorax and eight pairs in the abdomen. Oxygen is thus supplied directly to the organs of the body rather than being carried through the system by the blood, as in humans.

There are no red corpuscles in the life stream of the bee. Its blood is a colourless fluid which is pumped forward to the head and then flows backward through passages in the thorax and abdomen, re-entering the heart at the end of its journey. This heart is a long muscular tube, having four chambers and lying in the abdomen. The blood, as it courses through the body on its round trip, picks up food passed through the walls of the alimentary canal and carries this nourishment to the vital organs.

Because of the tremendous amount of energy used in flying, the bee requires quick assimilaton of its food. In addition, it must take nourishment at frequent intervals. Some years ago, a European scientist analysed the sugar content of the blood of the bee. For normal human beings, it is one-tenth of one per cent. For active honey gatherers, he found, it is twenty times as high, two per cent.

Running along the bottom of the rounded abdomen is a slight "keel" and on either side are the flat "wax plates." It is upon these plates that glands within the abdomen secrete the fluid that hardens into fish-scale-like flakes of wax. Back of these plates, at the tip of the pointed abdomen, you find the organ which is familiar to thousands of persons who know little else about this remarkable insect. This is the sting.

Without this weapon, with which to defend the collected honey, all the work of the bees would be undone. Despoilers would reap the reward of the industry and frugality of the honeybee colony. Left alone, the bee is almost always a good neighbour. It is only when it is disturbed or imagines it is being attacked that it uses its sting.

The sting itself, if we can view it without emotion, is one of the wonders of Nature's workshop. Sharp as the sharpest needle, hard almost as steel, it is barbed in the manner of a porcupine quill so it cannot be withdrawn, once it is inserted. Literally, it harms the bee more than it does you when she stings. For, in the act she loses her life. The whole end of the worker's abdomen is torn away when she attempts to withdraw the barbed spear of her sting. The queen has a curved, scimitar-like sting which is smooth and can be used over and over again. But she uses her weapon only on other queens and makes no effort to sting man. Drones have no stings at all.

This, then, is the worker bee: a half-inch creature bounded fore and aft by strange stick-like antennae—forming the nose of the insect—and the dreaded sting—by means of which it protects its hard-won stores. Between are the tools of the legs, the multi-cellular eyes, the curiously fashioned tongue, the transparent wings, the powerful muscles of the thorax, the tube-like four-chambered heart, the infinitely branched tracheae that make lungs unneeded, and the wax plates so vital to the building of comb.

To the bee, the world in which it lives is alternately the sunny fields and the close-packed darkness of the hive. It is a world of per-fumes and odours, of objects seen in ultra-violet light as well as in rays visible to our eyes; but a world in which greens and reds appear as grey: a world of delicately shaded differences in nectar taste; a world that is largely silence but filled with the mysterious language of vibration.

My bees, beginning the season of plenty with their joyous aerial dance beyond the window, are well equipped for the life they lead. Nature, through aeons of evolution, has given them the body, the senses, the instincts needed to make their waxen city a success. It was Jean Jacques Rousseau who once wrote: "An insect . . . whose strength exceeds its needs is strong; an elephant, a lion, a conqueror, a hero . . . whose needs exceed his strength is weak.

As weeks go by, and nectar comes to the full tide of its flood, the activity of the hive will rise to a crescendo. During the days when at millions of flowers bee-gold is to be had for the taking, my insects will earn to the full their reputation as a symbol for industry. These weeks of opulence and harvest are known to the beekeeeper by the picturesque and apt expression "honey flow."

5

HONEY FLOW

THIS morning I placed a bit of honey on the window sill within six inches of the entrance of my hive. All day the bees have streamed past without the slightest notice and now little red ants are busy harvesting the sweet which, another time, would have brought the bees clustering in great excitement. The explanation is simple. The honey flow is on. The harvest of the bees is in full swing. Meadows and fields and gardens are ablaze with nectar-filled blooms. Everywhere sweets are to be had for the taking.

In such times of honey flow, workers have been seen going afield in pouring rain when great drops struck with hammerlike blows on wings and bodies. On windy days, they alight on flowers that dart from side to side, lashed and shaken by gusts. I have seen my bees returning like laden vessels, tacking about and flying low in the teeth of an approaching windstorm.

During the height of the honey-making season, a foraging bee will work itself to death, literally, in six weeks. The classic experiments of Dr Jacques Loeb, at the University of Chicago, find a counterpart in the life of the hive. Dr Loeb, day after day, placed rats on treadmills that were turning at different rates of speed. The animals that ran on the most swiftly moving wheels had far shorter life spans than those that maintained a more leisurely pace. In other words, the length of the life of the individual rat depended upon how fast the life was lived. Similarly, among the bees, workers that are born in autumn live six months or more, using up comparatively little of their store of energy in winter, while the workers that emerge in summer, during the intense labour of the honey harvest, have a life span only a fraction as long.

In an isolated section of Wyoming some years ago, research scientists of the U.S. Department of Agriculture installed several beehives. The nearest source of nectar was an irrigated alfalfa field, eight miles away. The bees soon found the flowers and began making sixteen-mile round-trip flights to bring the nectar home. Calculations revealed the amazing fact that these half-inch insects were flying nearly 300,000 miles in storing up a single pound of honey. Even in regions where flowers abound, a pound of honey represents a combined flight mileage of approximately 50,000 miles, the equivalent of two circuits of the globe !

Thus one bee, working a lifetime, could never produce a pound of honey. As many as 37,000 loads of nectar may go into the production of this amount of concentrated sweets. According to the noted British scientist, J. Arthur Thomson, worker bees from one hive will visit more than a quarter of a million blooms in a single day. Returning home, with their tiny wings supporting a load of nectar equal to half the entire weight of the bee, my insects travel at a speed of about fifteen miles an hour. On long journeys, the laden bees stop for occasional rests. Sometimes, in crossing lakes and rivers, bees become exhausted, fall into the water, and drown.

In spite of the intense labour of their short lives, worker bees during honey flow always impart a curious, pervading sense of good cheer. It seems to me that no other living creature, with the possible exception of a swallow wheeling and skimming at dusk, combines so much pleasure with the task of making a living. "A bee among the flowers," says an old English writer, "is one of the cheerfulest objects that can be looked upon. Its life appears to be all enjoyment, *so busy and so pleased.*"

As I became more and more closely acquainted with the bees, I found they were capable of many variations. Individuals exhibited differences and peculiarities. Marked bees, I found, performed small tasks in their own way. They solved problems by the trial-and-error method. They learned by experience.

Dr Frank E. Lutz, of the American Museum of Natural History, has shown that bees will turn upside down and assume unnatural positions in order to pass through a trap door into a chamber that holds sweets. Bees will learn to visit flowers they ordinarily avoid as soon as tiny amounts of honey are placed daily in the blooms. I have seen honeybees using the holes that bumblebees have bitten through the sides of honeysuckle blossoms to obtain nectar which ordinarily they could not reach. Even more striking is the manner in which bees have learned the right time of day to visit buckwheat fields. The flowers of these plants close their nectaries after ten o'clock in the morning. You find the bees humming about the flowers early in the morning but wasting little or no time among the fields of buckwheat after midday.

The flight of a foraging bee is far from a haphazard affair. If I could follow one of the insects now darting away into the sunshine, I would find it moving from one flower to another of the same species. If it is gathering apple-blossom nectar, it will pass over whole gardens of iris, whole fields of dandelions, without stopping at a single bloom. When it returns, its honey bag is filled with nectar from a single kind of flower. It is this fact that makes the honeybee such an invaluable ally of the plant world. It carries pollen to the blooms that can use it, the flowers of the same species. Without bees of all kinds to pollinate their blooms, it is estimated, 100,000 species of plants would disappear from the earth.

Flowers that are pollinated by the wind instead of by bees and other insects are usually small, dull-coloured or green, and without both nectar and perfume. Nectar is the fee paid by the plant for the fertilizing service of the insect. Yet, according to E. R. Root, as much as ninety per cent of all the nectar in the eastern part of the

United States goes to waste because there are not enough bees to harvest it. In the west, where the nectar supplies as a rule are less varied, a more thorough harvest is made. Honeybees in a Colorado desert, for instance, have been observed gathering nectar from plants so tiny that a magnifying glass is required to see the flowers distinctly.

The elder Pliny, in Roman times, wrote of foraging bees: "They do not go from their hive more than three-score paces ; and if it chance that they do not find sufficient flowers within these limits, out go their spies whom they send to discover forage further off. If, in this expedition, they are overtaken by night, they crouch upon their back for fear lest their wings should be overcharged with the evening dew."

Little more exact information than that was known about the habits of bees for seventeen centuries after Pliny. Then came the experiments of Réaumur, Huber, and Lubbock, made in the modern scientific manner, and finally, as late as in the 1930's, the brilliant work of Karl von Frisch, at the University of Munich, Germany. The results of his ingenious and exhaustive tests reveal what this careful scientist describes as "The Language of the Bees."

Men had often wondered since Pliny's time how the spy, or scout, bees report their finds. How do they communicate to other members of the colony the location of the flowers they discover? And how do these bees recognize desirable blooms amid flower-filled fields?

To begin with, von Frisch studied the senses of the bee, repeating some of the experiments of Lubbock and other investigators, and devising new ones of his own. On a small table in the meadow of the Munich Botanical Gardens, he placed a square of blue cardboard. On this square he laid a watch-crystal dish, holding a dab of honey. Soon, bees were alighting, sucking up the honey, and flying away. A few days later, when the insects had become accustomed to the place, he removed the honey, the dish, and the cardboard square. On either side of the spot where the blue cardboard had been, he placed two new squares, one red, the other blue. Would the bees, remembering the place where they had obtained the honey, alight between the coloured squares? Would they become confused and alight, some on one square and some on the other? Or would they recognize the blue colour and alight exclusively on it?

The scientist watched closely and saw the returning insects veer to the blue cardboard. They had demonstrated that they could remember colour. Next he placed the blue cardboard in the midst of grey cardboards that ranged from almost black to almost white. If the bees were colour-blind to blue and had picked it out merely because it was a different shade of grey from the red square, they would be confused by the grey cards. Unhesitatingly, the insects alighted on the blue square. Yellow, violet, purple, orange, were tried out in the same manner and the bees showed they could recognize and remember each hue. Red, von Frisch found, could not be distinguished from grey. The bees were colour-blind to red. In this connection, it is interesting to note that rarely do bees visit red flowers. Among blooms of this hue, fertilization is accomplished most often by hummingbirds and butterflies rather than by bees.

When von Frisch spread cardboard squares of all the different colours on his table, he discovered that the bees had difficulty in distinguishing yellow from orange and blue from purple. In summing up the results of his tests, he found that although the insects are colour-blind to red and cannot distinguish as many shades of colour as we can, they are able to remember and recognize many hues. This ability undoubtedly plays a part in aiding them in their search for specific blooms.

So much for colour sense. Next the scientist studied their sense of smell. The cardboard squares were replaced by small pasteboard boxes, each having a little hole in the front. Von Frisch attempted to train the bees to scent just as he had trained them to colour. Several boxes were placed on the table. Only one contained a watch-crystal dish with honey in it: the others were empty. And that one also held a drop of penetrating perfume. The bees soon found the honey. Then the position of the boxes was changed. Still they unhesitatingly approached the perfumed container, ignoring the others. This box was removed and another, perfumed but holding no food, was put among the other boxes. The bees immediately entered it, guided by smell. Between thirty and forty different perfumes were tried. The result was the same. The bees could recognize and remember each scent, just as they could remember shades of colour.

Thus in the field, the scout bee is equipped with eyes that can recognize the colour of a flower at some distance and a sense of smell that can make the recognition complete at close range. For different species of flowers have their own distinctive perfumes. This explains how the foraging bee can hum from flower to flower, keeping to the same species, in a wide field gay with vari-coloured blooms.

This, however, was only the beginning of von Frisch's work. The most fascinating part of the researches was yet to come. He had often noticed that shortly after one bee found the honey on his observation table, scores of other bees, always from the same hive, appeared on the spot. The original discoverer must have communicated news of his find to the other bees of the colony. How? This was the mystery that the scientist set out to clear up.

First he worked out an elaborate coloured-spot code for numbering bees. A white spot on the front of the thorax represented the number one, a red spot number two, an orange spot number three, a yellow spot number four, a green spot number five. Placed on other parts of the body, the dabs of colours represented other numbers. Thus it was possible to mark 599 bees each with a distinctive number that could be seen even when the insect was in flight and could be recognized at a glance when the bee was at the table or inside the glass walls of an observation hive. Following a marked bee from the honey on the table to the hive, von Frisch watched its actions closely after it arrived on the comb.

First it delivered the honey to other bees. Then it began a curious dance, "turning round and round in a circle with quick, tripping little steps, once to the right, once to the left, very vigorously." Often the dance was repeated several times on several spots. The bees around became greatly excited. "They tripped behind the dancer, following all its turning movements. They turned their heads to it and kept their feelers as close as possible to its body. Then, suddenly, one of the following bees turned aside, cleaned its antennae, and left the hive. Others did the same." And not long afterward, these new bees appeared at the table where the honey was found. By means of its strange dance in the midst of the other bees, the insect that discovered the sweets had communicated the news. But how had the later arrivals found their way to the spot?

At first von Frisch thought the original bee led them. But he soon found they arrived individually, minutes apart. A further experiment solved the riddle. Moving his feeding table to within forty feet, due west, of the hive, the scientist placed on it a dish containing sugar water and honey. One of the marked bees discovered it, returned to the hive, and performed the honey dance. In the meantime, von Frish had placed dishes of similar sugar water and honey on the meadow to the east, north, west, and south of the hive. If the language of the dance told the other bees exactly where to go, they would all come to the table. But this did not happen. The experimenter found that the dishes lying at all points of the compass from the hive were found just as quickly as was the one on the feeding table. The dance had told the bees only that the food was available. They had to fly out in all directions and look for it.

Under natural conditions, however, the scientist found, bees receive additional help in this search. Putting the glass dishes away, von Frisch turned to flowers, the familiar source of nectar. He placed a large bunch of cyclamen on his table and beside it a bunch of phlox. With a medicine dropper, he added sugar water to the nectar of the cyclamen blooms to provide an ample supply of food. Bees, finding the sweets, returned to the hive and performed the honey dance. Shortly afterward other bees were alighting on the cyclamen and paying no attention to the near-by phlox. This, of course, is not surprising, because bees cannot get honey from phlox and almost never visit them. But this fact makes the next step in the experiment all the more effective.

The flowers at the feeding station were changed. This time, extra sweets were placed in the phlox and the nectar largely removed from the cyclamen. Homing bees carried the news and there followed the strange sight of new bees alighting on the scorned phlox and paying not the slightest attention to the familiar cyclamen. More than that, all over the surrounding territory bees from the hive were investigating phlox, seemingly puzzled by the fact that they found no food! Thus, von Frisch demonstrated, in natural life, the dancing bee reports in addition to the fact that there is food, the kind of flower in which it will be found.

A clue as to how this was done was found in the fact that the experiments with flowers succeeded for all kinds except those which had no scent. The conclusion is obvious. The perfume of the flower adheres to the body of the bee which enters it to obtain the nectar. During the dance at the home hive, the antennae of the surrounding bees pick up this scent message and when they leave the hive, they are searching for a flower with a definite scent.

By substituting bits of perfumed cardboard for flowers, von

Frisch easily proved that this was so. Over the meadow, he scattered a number of pieces of cardboard holding various perfumes. At the feeding table, he gave sugar water to a marked bee by means of a watch-crystal dish placed on a piece of cardboard, scented with perfume. The bee which reported the find, carried the scent with it into the hive. A few minutes later, other bees appeared at the cardboard on the table. But still others were alighting on cards having the identical scent among the scattered bits of paste-board on the meadow. They ignored the squares with different perfumes and descended only where the familiar odour issued from the grass.

Thus, action and scent and taste play leading roles in the language of the bees. One step farther in his researches demonstrated to von Frisch that the insects possess some way of governing the number of additional bees that flock to a reported feeding place. If there is only a slight surplus, a few new bees come; if the new source of food appears unlimited, many appear at the spot. What is the explanation?

By watching his marked bees through the glass walls of his observation hive, the experimenter discovered the simple answer. When the feeding table held a large dish of sugar water, the bees that returned danced also. They attracted others from the colony, just as they had been attracted by the original discoverer. But when the amount of food was reduced, the incoming bees simply delivered the sweets without calling out additional workers. In this way, the number of bees in a given area can be controlled during honey flow. If there are too few bees among certain flowers, the returning workers dance and other bees join them in their work; if too many bees are labouring in the area and the nectar supply begins to fail, the dancing stops.

The same procedure applies to the richness of the nectar. If one kind of flower is producing very sweet nectar and another flower nectar that is watery and diluted, the bees collecting the former will dance and attract more workers. In this way, the efforts of the colony are spent where the profit is greatest.

A few years ago, a curious instance of this ability of the bees to concentrate their efforts where the rewards are greatest was reported from Kentucky. A farmer took seventy-five pounds of surplus honey from his hives and stored it in a garage not far from the beeyard. The insects discovered this rich mine of concentrated sweets. They gave up visiting flowers and devoted all their time to the honey. Before the farmer discovered what they were doing, they had transported almost the whole seventy-five pounds back to the hives again!

When the honey flow is on in full force and many kinds of flowers are blooming at once, scout bees that discover the best nectar attract the most workers to that type of bloom. Here taste also plays its part in the language of the bees. Von Frisch found that he could increase or decrease the vigour of the dance on the comb of the hive merely by increasing or decreasing the sugar content of his feeding syrups at the observation table.

A flower is a flower and a weed a weed only in the sight of man. To the bee, all blooming plants are rated by a simple and basic measurement: the amount of nectar, and the quality of the sweet they produce. It was Charles Darwin who remarked that bees must be good botanists because they are able to recognize related species of plants that provide good nectar supplies.

Throughout the honey flow, the bees are working at peak speed. They hum away into the sunshine only to reappear again bearing their load of liquid gold. Even during the homeward flight, the complex chemical change which transforms the nectar of the flower into the honey of the hive is beginning to take place. How the transformation is completed within the treasure vaults of the bees and the magic by which these hexagonal cells are created is the story of the ensuing chapter.

6

TREASURE VAULTS

HONEY, to the golden throng, represents life. It means food and warmth in months of cold. It is the link between the years, the basis of survival. Such liquid gold is more than ordinary gold, more than a symbol of wealth or a medium of exchange; it is wealth itself—edible, life-giving, fundamental wealth.

If you collected nectar from the identical flowers the bees are visiting and let the water evaporate, you would not have honey. Chemical change, occurring within the body of the insect, is essential to the transformation.

As soon as one of my bees sucks nectar into its honey bag or crop, the chemical factory within its body begins to function. Enzymes, complex organic substances believed to originate in the salivary glands, mix with the nectar. While the bee flies homeward, the sugar of the nectar is being converted into the dextrose and levulose of honey. At the hive, the nectar load is transferred to the crops of younger workers. These bees force it in and out of their bodies several times in what appears to be a thorough mixing process. Then they store the rather thin, partially ripened honey in open cells. Currents of air, produced by fanning wings, evaporate the excess water from the fluid. When it has reached the composition and consistency of honey, it is capped with wax. Thus the harvest of the bees proceeds. It is an infinitely more complex process than simply gathering nectar in the honey flow.

According to chemists of the U.S. Department of Agriculture, average American honey contains: water, 17.70 per cent; levulose, 40.50 per cent; dextrose, 34.02 per cent; cane sugar, 1.90 per cent; dextrins and gums, 1.51 per cent; ash, 0.15 per cent. Besides, there are small quantities of bees-wax, a few pollen grains suspended in the honey, and colouring material from the plants which supplied the nectar.

The hue of honey, familiarly yellow, may range all the way from wine-red in the Appalachian tupelo-tree region to yellowish-green in the star-thistle country of California. Among the most famous American honeys are the amber-white clover honey of the Middle West, the sparkling sage honey of the Far West, and the delicately flavoured orange-blossom honey of Florida and California.

No matter what its hue or flavour, honey is a concentrated carbo-hydrate food of many uses. Physicians have prescribed it for feeding infants and for the diet of typhoid patients. It is considered a blood builder and a quick source of energy. Honey is mildly laxative and is noted for its soothing effect in cough medicines. Cosmetics sometimes contain it. It was widely used in both the honey wine of Rome and the mead of mediaeval Europe. And the Egyptians at one time employed this product of the bees as an embalming fluid.

About fifty per cent heavier than water and possessing both a higher boiling point and a lower freezing point, honey is a fluid of many mysteries. For example, when a cane-sugar solution of the same density and the same number of molecules as honey is frozen, it becomes a solid mass. Honey, however, reacts differently. It remains mushy and is still capable of flowing slowly. Because of this property, honey has at times been used as a makeshift anti-freeze fluid in automobile radiators.

Another puzzling feature is the vast difference in viscosity in various kinds of honey. Some types are almost watery, while the celebrated heather honey of Europe is so viscous you can turn a jar of it upside down and the contents will not flow out. Yet chemists who have examined this heather honey have found it contains a higher water content than other types that flow more easily.

Ordinary honey will flow rather freely, especially when it is first made. The reason it does not run out of the comb is that each cell is tilted slightly upward. The outer end is just enough higher than the inner end to keep the honey within. This is but one of the striking features found in the wax comb which provides treasure vaults for the hive.

So strong is the fragile-appearing honeycomb, with its cell walls sometimes only two one-thousandths of an inch thick, that one pound of comb will support twenty-five pounds or more of honey. The production of this wonder of wax is an achievement of co-operation and instinct.

As you watch the process, you see the wax-making workers cluster together in a golden mass. Heat is essential to the production of this building material of the bees. Within the bunches and festoons of insects, the temperature rises to approximately ninety-seven degrees F. As time passes, little glands on the lower side of the abdomen of the bees begin to secrete a fluid which hardens on contact with the air. Thus, on the eight wax plates of the last four segments of the abdomen, there appear flat, almost transparent pieces of wax, suggesting fish scales. The plastic material they provide forms the fundamental building substance of the insect city. Without it, all the industry and all the thrift of the golden throng would be to no avail.

Early naturalists supposed that wax was obtained, as nectar is, directly from flowers. Huber, with typical straightforward common sense, proved by a simple experiment that the insects create the wax instead of obtaining it from flowers or plants. He fed imprisoned bees on a pure sugar-solution diet and found they produced wax as easily as when foraging afield for their food.

Propolis, the dark bee glue with which the insects fill cracks and smooth over rough places within the hive, is obtained from the gums of buds and plants and trees. But wax is a product of the same chemical factory that changes nectar into honey—the body of the worker bee. It is a by-product of metabolism. To create one pound of wax, recent tests have shown, bees must consume six or seven pounds of honey.

Although the other social honey makers, the bumblebees and the stingless bees, both produce wax, its chemical composition is different. In the laboratory a chemist can distinguish between the wax of the honeybee and that of the bumblebee, for instance, without difficulty. Also, among bumblebees, queens and workers produce wax from gland pockets on both the top and bottom of the abdomen. Honeybees have these glands on the lower side of the abdomen, while the stingless bees have them only on the upper side. However, among the latter insects, the queens and the drones, as well as the workers, produce the scales of plastic building material. Among the hive bees, wax seems to be produced mainly by the younger workers before they begin making nectar-gathering trips afield. Later, the wax glands appear to degenerate so that older bees are unable to produce these tiny wafers which form the white "building bricks" of the hive.

In olden times, these flakes of wax were often referred to as "the fat of the bees." Although beeswax is somewhat allied to fats in its atomic make-up, it is unlike anything else in the world. Some of its constituents are: a fatty acid called cerin, minute quantities of alcohol, myricin, hydrocarbons, and an acid which gives the wax its characteristic odour.

Unlike honey, beeswax is lighter than water and floats. Resistant to heat, it will endure temperatures up to 140 degrees F. before it melts. No other wax known has so high a melting point. I have seen pictures of beeswax candles remaining upright with a thermometer beside them registering a summer heat of 110 degrees. This characteristic of wax is of utmost importance to the little builders within the hive. They would lose their whole store of liquid gold if the thin-walled treasure vaults in which it is stored softened and gave way.

Beeswax, in fact, is just as strange and interesting a solid as honey is a fluid. Its unusual properties have made it useful in an infinite number of ways in the world of men as well as of bees. This wax is employed in lubricants, in salves, in ointments, in harness oils, in gramophone records, in sealing wax, in furniture polish, and in some types of varnishes. Electrical coils sometimes use it as an insulator. The finest candles are made from beeswax. And, at the present time, more than half a million pounds a year go into the production of comb foundations which apiarists place in the hives, permitting the bees to build up the sides of the cells and thus save valuable time for nectar hunting. In fact, so varied and extensive is the demand for beeswax that the production in the United States is insufficient to meet the need. Some years, as much as 5,000,000 pounds have been imported from abroad.

But to return to the source of this valuable material, the wax plates of the bees. By means of the spines on the rear legs—the same ones the insect uses as pollen combs—the bee pries loose the eight scales, one after the other. It passes each forward to the front legs. Holding it up to its jaws, it chews the wax, minute after minute. The scale, when it leaves the wax plate, is almost transparent, like a bit of mica. As the bee chews it, something akin to the beating of the white of an egg takes place. Air bubbles enter the substance and from an almost transparent scale it turns into a white mass—the material of which the hexagonal comb-cells are built.

The manner in which the insects carry the prepared wax to the place of its use varies with the circumstances. Ordinarily, it is held in the jaws. But according to many watchers, when a worker bee has to carry the prepared wax some distance, it "slips it under its chin," so to speak. If, during its flight, the material begins to slide out of place, the insect quickly raises a foreleg and tucks it back. When the little wafer of wax reaches its destination, it is still warm and soft, ready for use.

Each bee, you will notice, uses only the wax it produces itself. Sometimes little scales, which have been dropped by the clustering bees, will be found strewing the bottom of the hive, unused. These scales, as they come from the wax plates, are usually pear-shaped and rather brittle. It is by means of the chewing process that the bees make the material pliable and ready for use. Honey flow and swarming time, naturally, are periods when wax making reaches a maximum. If bees are fed artificially for several days, so that the food supply suddenly increases, they are likely to begin making wax. Thus Nature provides for the necessity of new and additional storage vaults. The production of wax rises and falls with the rise and fall of the nectar tide.

Constructing the cells of the comb is a task that brings the bees to the peak of their co-operative efficiency. First, you see a few bees deposit bits of the white, masticated wax in approximately the right place. Other bees follow in rapid succession. Workers give the plastic material successive pinches with their mandibles. The mass begins to take shape. Perfect six-sided cells grow before your eye—marvels of economy and engineering skill. The hexagonal form of the honeycomb cell provides the maximum strength, the greatest storage space, and, at the same time, suits the cylindrical body of the grub and nymph.

Some scientists have maintained that the cells of the comb are really round; that the six-sided appearance is the result of the close juxtaposition of the cylinders, just as though you were to place scores of round pencils, pushed close together, into a mass of clay. However, plaster-of-paris models and samples of comb in

TEACHABLE. Scientists have proved they can teach bees, by placing extra nectar in blooms, to visit regularly flowers which they ordinarily avoid.

TINY FLOWERS, such as these blooms of the purple vetch, are none too small for the honeybee to visit during its foraging flights afield.

PUSSYWILLOW POLLEN is gathered by bees early in spring for feeding the larvae. Because it is rich in protein, pollen is vital to brood-rearing.

BEAUTY of flowers is one by-product of the pollenizing activity of honeybees. It is estimated that if all kinds of bees were destroyed, 100,000 varieties of flowering plants would disappear from the earth.

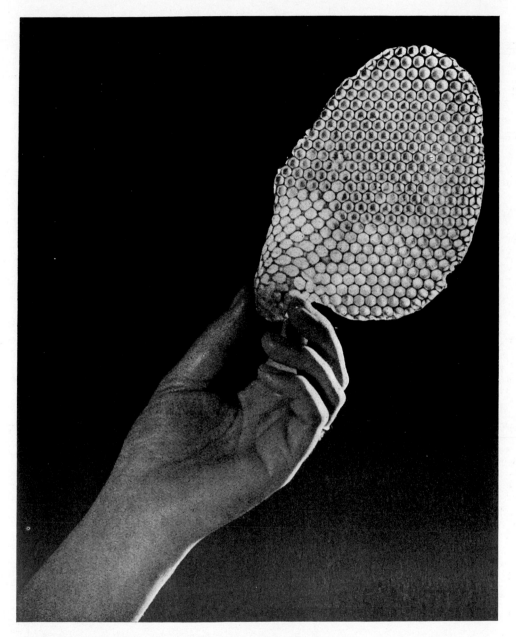

A MASTERPIECE OF ART AND ENGINEERING, the wax comb of the honeybee is able to support twenty-five times its own weight, in spite of the fact that the walls of its hexagonal cells often are only $\frac{2}{1000}$ of an inch thick.

OPEN-AIR COMBS are sometimes constructed by the bees of a swarm when they alight on a branch and then are held up by bad weather. Such a colony is doomed unless it is placed in a hive before the arrival of the winter cold.

SKEP COMB, attached to the inside of an old-fashioned straw skep, is anchored to the dome-shaped hive and so cannot be removed for examination as can the frames of the Langstroth hive, now most widely used.

MOUNTAINS OF WAX, such as the above, are created in the hive from secretions of tiny glands located in the abdomen of the worker bees. Younger members of the colony make most of the wax.

FOUNDATION for honeycomb, pressed from wax, saves time for the bees and enables them to spend more hours hunting nectar.

SIX SIDED. The plaster cast, top, and three stages in comb construction, left to right, show hexagonal development of the cells.

A WAX PEANUT is what the queen cell suggests at first glance. As many as a dozen of these pendant cells are sometimes created by bees in a single hive during spring weeks when the honey flow is unusually heavy.

THE FOUNDATION of the queen cell, attached to the side or bottom of the regular brood comb, looks like the dark cap of an acorn.

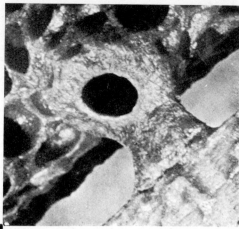

FINISHING TOUCHES are placed on the cell by worker bees which cover the exterior with a thick and roughened coating of wax.

EMPTY cells often have the circular cap, pushed outward by the emerging queen, still attached like a door swinging on its hinges.

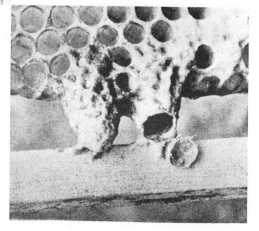

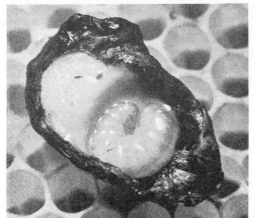

ROYAL JELLY nourishes the queen larva within the cell. This concentrated gland food hastens development of the grub.

ROYAL NYMPH. Such maturing queens have been kept in glass vials by scientists who studied the details of their growth.

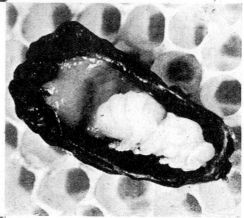

ROYAL BEE. The instinctive act of the emerging queen is to hunt down and slay, in their cells, her unborn rivals.

TWO ENEMIES of the honeybee are the dragonfly and the toad. Toads have been seen eating an average of more than twenty bees an evening and dragonflies once destroyed $1,000 worth of queens at a Florida apiary.

FEARSOME FOE. The praying mantis, found in eastern and southern U.S.A., gets its name from its habit of raising forelegs, as though in prayer, while awaiting the approach of a victim. It catches harmful pests more often than bees.

THE WAX MOTH, top, lays eggs in the hive. Grubs hatch out and, eating wax as they go, produce silk-lined tunnels, bottom, that ruin the comb.

A MOUSE NEST, found in a hive at the end of the winter season, is large enough to fill a half-bushel basket.

PROPOLIS, or bee-glue, as it appears after it has been used by the insects for smoothing the interior of a hive.

THE QUEEN'S COURT attends her night and day. These worker bees surround her in an oval, always facing her. When she pauses in egg laying, the members of the court quickly press close, cleaning and feeding her.

various stages of completion show that the cells are built up from the beginning with six definite walls of wax.

Not all cells, however, are hexagonal. Bees are able to take care of emergencies. Sometimes they instinctively build triangular, square, or other odd-shaped cells to fill in unusual spaces. But the ordinary honeycomb is formed with such unvarying accuracy that at one time the French scientist, Réaumur, proposed the cell of the hive bee as a standard measure. We know now that the exact dimensions of these hexagonal vaults will vary slightly under different conditions. But the average is amazingly uniform.

An instance which illustrates this fact was related to me by a New York diemaker. Some time ago, he was commissioned to produce a zinc die for pressing honeycomb into the foundations used in bee hives. The die was completed; the comb foundations made. Then it was discovered the bees refused to use them. A checkup revealed that the workman who had laid out the die had been off on his cell dimensions a tiny fraction of an inch. When the die was redesigned and the error eliminated, the insects accepted the new foundations and built their cells upon them.

The cells of the comb have a twofold use. They provide storage space for the honey and cradles for the maturing bees. When brood cells are used for storing honey, they are often lengthened to increase their capacity. The cells of the brood comb, if you run your eye across an expanse of them, will be found to be of two sizes. The larger ones, running about four cells to the inch, are for the drones; the more numerous ones, averaging a fraction more than five cells to the inch, are for the workers. The latter cradles are almost invariably seven-eighths of an inch in length.

Pure white at first, the wax in honeycomb becomes tarnished to yellow. In brood comb, it becomes a chocolate brown that is almost black. Built so it hangs vertically, with cells back to back to form a double layer, the brood comb of the hive represents a vast hanging insect skyscraper with thousands of adjoining apartments.

How do the little insect engineers that produce this marvel of wax calculate their dimensions with such exactness? What yard-stick do they use? How do they, working apparently at random— one giving the wax a pinch, then another—achieve cells that are perfect hexagons, that are just the size needed, that are tilted at just the right angle to prevent thin honey from running out? Theirs is an achievement of co-operative construction the wonder of which grows with contemplation.

7

ENEMIES

ONE evening, Samuel Johnson and his biographer, Boswell, were discussing the vast estates of an English lord.

"One should think," remarked Boswell, "that the proprietor of all this *must* be happy.

"Nay," Johnson replied, "all this excludes but one evil—poverty."

So with the wealth of the bees. The row on row of waxen treasure vaults solves only part of the problems of existence. The stores of these hard-working insects attract rather than repel a host of predatory rovers. In short, as an old writer of the sixteenth century puts it, the bees, like many good people, have many bad enemies.

They have enemies in fur, in feathers, in scales, in the armour of the insects. They have enemies that crawl, that walk, that fly. They have enemies that mimic the sound of the queen, that attach themselves to the bodies of the workers, that use almost incredibly cunning ruses for gaining entrance into the stronghold of the hive. Their foes range from the almost microscopic bee louse and an even smaller nite to the huge and shaggy bear; from tiny beetles to man himself.

Late one June morning, as I was watching the activity within the glass house of my bees, their low, calm humming suddenly rose to an excited pitch. Workers ran rapidly this way and that. They milled about in angry activity. A number converged on the entrance. Small, dark specks, moving along the bottom of the comb, explained their sudden change in temper. The hive had been invaded by minute red ants.

Only a few of the intruders had gained an entrance and the doorway was soon guarded by an almost solid mass of bees. In some cases, when tiny ants swarm over the comb in a mass invasion, the bees, finding they cannot sting their midget foes, pick them up bodily and, flying a distance from the hive, drop them on the ground.

Ants, insects so fond of sweets that they often guard plant lice in order to lick up the honeydew the aphides give off, are frequent invaders of hives, particularly in warm or tropical regions. In some cases, ants and bees have been known to engage in deadly warfare, the bees seeking to use their stings and the ants trying to bite off the wings and legs of their adversaries. Most of these attacks are made at night. Sometimes the dead bodies of the combatants will litter the ground about the entrance of the hive under such conditions. Unless the beekeeper comes to the rescue of his insects, the ants destroy the colony and plunder the hard-earned stores of the bees.

The Argentine ant of the Southern states, instead of trying to force an entrance at the doorway, simply eats its way through the bottom board of the hive. Southern apiarists, and those who raise bees in the tropics, outwit the ants by placing the hives on short poles which hold a ring of sticky pitch or similar material near the base to prevent the ants from reaching the honey above. This tanglefoot strip is often replaced by a more permanent form of protection, a cuplike piece of metal running around the post and filled with creosote, coal tar, or crude petroleum.

Some enemies of the bees enter the hive for other purposes than to plunder the stores of honey. One of the strangest of these robber foes—the larva of the common European oil beetle—comes in search of honeybee eggs. This larva hatches out far from the hive, amid decaying leaves where the female beetle lays her minute eggs. It slowly crawls up the stem of some flowering plant, patiently awaits the coming of a honeybee, and then fastens itself to the body of the winged insect. Sailing through the air as the bee flies from flower to flower, the amazing little passenger finally reaches it goal.

In the hive, it lets go its hold and creeps into the cells where eggs have been deposited by the queen. Feeding on an exclusive diet of honeybee eggs, it grows until its skin splits and it molts and becomes a larger larva. From then on, it is a honey eater. When the end of its larval period is come, it changes into an adult beetle and sails away on its own wings. The females lay other eggs in leafy debris and the whole fantastic life story begins again.

Another curious invader of the hive is the louse of the honeybee, *Braula coeca*. Pale, almost transparent, this tiny wingless fly clings tightly to the body of the bee to which it attaches itself. Once I saw half a dozen of these minute creatures leaving the body of a dead bee, almost as though waxen scales were falling away. In earlier days, it was thought the bee lice, like the lice that cling to the bodies of mammals, sucked vital juices from the bees. More recent researches into the life history of this minute parasite have shown that its food consists largely of nectar and honey which it removes from the mouth parts of its host. The larvae of these honeybee lice do far more damage than the adults. They hatch from eggs laid in the wax capping over the cells of honey. Immediately they begin to tunnel back and forth inside the capping material. The diameter of the tunnels increases as the larva grows larger. Beekeepers have found that this tiny invader of the hive—which is found in only a few parts of the country—can easily be killed by tobacco smoke.

Far more destructive are the tunnels of another larva, the child of the wax moth, *Galleria mellonella*. Early on an evening in summer, these dusty yellow moths can be seen circling about the hive in the twilight, seeking to gain an entrance. They are about the size of the familiar "dusty miller," and often are called the "moth miller" or the "bee moth." The larva is known colloquially as the "wax worm."

Invading the hive of a weak colony, the moth lays its eggs in crevices from which the hatching wax worms crawl to begin their tunnel building. The oddity of the diet of this larva puzzled scientists for many years. It apparently thrives on the non-nitrogenous carbon compound, wax, in spite of the fact that no animal can live without some supply of vital nitrogen. The explanation seems to be that it picks up bits of pollen grains and parts of dead bees as it progresses through the wax of the comb.

During this progress, it spins a silken web that lines the tunnel it makes. The winding trail of one of these larvae is easily distinguished at a glance. I have seen combs where the sides of the open cells have been eaten away almost to the foundation by the bees in their effort to reach and destroy the tunnel maker.

In Europe, the death's-head sphinx moth, a twilight insect with dark markings suggesting a death's head on its back, is a dreaded enemy of the hive. The name *propolis*, which has been given the resinous bee glue, comes from the Greek and refers to ramparts in front of a city. The word is said to have been chosen to designate bee glue as a result of the old-time belief that the bees often build a fortifying mound of this material at the door of their hive in order to prevent the bulky death's-head moth from gaining an entrance. Early writers often told how the adult moth imitated the piping of the queen and thus was assisted in gaining admittance to the interior. Her larvae, spinning their webs about the hive, greatly interfere with the work of the colony. Originally these moths of the twilight were mistaken for bats, which were long believed to invade the hive in search of honey.

Still another moth, the Mediterranean flour moth, comes to the hive to rob the "pantry cells" near the brood comb. Its larva eats the pollen stored up for feeding the grubs of the bees.

Small spiders, which invade the hive, have a plus and a minus after their entry as bee enemies. They sometimes catch bees but also sometimes kill the wax moths that enter the hive. So one activity may balance the other.

So much for the invaders. They, however, comprise only part of the enemy forces the bees must combat. When a nectar hunter darts away from the landing stage of the hive, it is like some little vessel setting sail on a pirate-infested sea. Perils lurk in the way. Orb spiders have stretched their sticky mazes across the beeways between the flowers; robber flies sweep down like insect falcons ; ambush bugs lie in wait among the petals of the blooms.

Even before it leaves its doorstep, a honeybee may fall victim to the common garden toad. This friend of the farmer, consuming 10,000 kinds of agricultural pests, may become itself a pest to the apiculturist. In researches made at the University of California, it was discovered that toads swarmed around bee hives on hot summer evenings, snapping up the bees that were fanning at the entrance. The scientists tabulated the catch of each toad. They found that the average was more than twenty bees a night.

In southern California, small lizards, as well as toads, prey on the hive dwellers. These little reptiles have been seen following a curious and ingenious procedure. Snapping up the bees by the forepart of their bodies, the lizards would swing their heads from side to side, rubbing the sting-bearing tails of the insects on the ground until they were damaged beyond the possibility of use. With nothing more to fear from its prey, the lizard then dined on its body at leisure.

The common skunk, one of several four-footed enemies of the

hive, has a somewhat similar way of dealing with bees. This animal has been seen approaching an isolated hive in the moonlight. Scratching on the side, it arouses the bees. Guards begin pouring out. As each one leaves the hive, the skunk deftly and swiftly rolls it back and forth on the ground, damaging its wings and putting it out of the combat.

For many years, the familiar kingbird was listed as a serious foe of the honeybee. It has been observed many times swooping down from a near-by perch to catch bees on the wing. So bad was its reputation at one time that its common name was "the bee martin." Late studies made by ornithologists have indicated that its consumption of bees has been greatly overrated and that, while it eats some bees, its damage to a colony is slight.

Far greater is the menace of hawking dragonflies. In five days, dragonflies once inflicted $1,000 damage on a single queen-rearing apiary in Florida. In some regions of the South, these "bee hawks" make queen raising almost impossible. It has been noted that when the dragonflies appear in zigzagging flocks near an apiary, the bees themselves sense the danger and remain in the hive instead of going afield for nectar and pollen. The dragonflies, catching sight of bees through their great multilensed eyes, dart toward them with their six spiny legs held together in the form of a basket. Without pausing, they scoop up the victims and often devour them on the wing.

Another insect that drops like a falcon on foraging bees is the robber fly. It selects some perch on a dead twig or weed top and from this lookout preys on the passing insects. I have spent hours watching the forays of these predatory flies. With great eyes that cover almost their entire heads, they keep vigilant watch. I have seen them dart away in a flash to snatch out of the air mosquitoes, small moths, flies, and tiny wasps, as well as bees. Their long legs are fitted with twin hooklike claws, sharp as needles. The fly wraps these legs about the flying victim, sinking the "talons" into its body. Then it returns to the perch to drain away the vital juices of its prey. A sliding lancet in the fly's projecting beak slits the chitin shell of the bee and enables it to insert its sucking proboscis into the soft interior. When all of the blood and softer tissues have been removed, the body of the victim falls to the ground, turning over and over like an empty bag.

Sometimes, beneath the lookout twig of one of these insect falcons, you can see the husks of a dozen or more honeybees, the empty bodies of luckless workers whose path carried them too close to the watch-tower twig of their enemy. One such "bee killer" is an almost perfect imitation of a large and hairy bumblebee. The more common robber flies are brown or grey, with bodies that are tapered and streamlined like racing airplanes.

In Southern and Eastern states, the enemy legions of the honeybee contain that curious, fascinating insect—a creature that seems to belong to another age or world—the praying mantis. Almost as long as your hand, and just the right shade of green or brown to camouflage it among leaves, it lies in wait for its victims. Harmless to man, it is often of great aid to the farmer because of the agricultural pests it devours. But in the eyes of the honeybee it is a fearsome foe.

Waiting with spiked forelegs lifted as though in an attitude of prayer, it remains motionless until a victim comes within reach. Then, with a lightning movement, the forelegs dart out and snap shut over the back of the bee. The spikes hold it as though it were imprisoned in a toothed steel trap, while the mantis dines on its helpless victim. Almost invariably it begins its meal by biting into the main nervous system, just behind the head. I have watched these creatures lie in wait for and trap such varied victims as hornets, wasps, bumblebees, dragonflies, caterpillars, beetles, and swallowtail butterflies.

A friend of mine once noticed one of these insects poised quietly on the top of a rosebush. Suddenly it darted its fore-legs up into the air with a movement almost too fast for the eye to follow. A honeybee which, an instant before, had been hovering above a bloom, disappeared in the wink of an eye, pulled down and imprisoned within the spiked forelegs of the mantis.

In the warm afternoons of Indian summer, yellow jackets often haunt the beeyards. I have seen as many as half a dozen of these wasps dining on one unfortunate drone which the workers had driven out of the hive to perish.

When short winter days have succeeded the lingering warmth of autumn and the bees have drawn together in their tight-packed cluster on the comb, another enemy of the bees, the furry, bright-eyed mouse, sometimes invades the hive. Here it builds its nest and dines on food it finds within. One nest of the kind, I once saw, was as large as a half-bushel basket. It was formed of tiny shreds of cloth brought in from the outside, and throughout the mass were the scattered bodies of dead bees.

Occasionally, in their effort to gain an entrance to the hive, mice arouse the fury of the insects and on various occasions they have been found stung to death. The body of such a creature, of course, cannot be removed from the hive. Consequently, the bees sometimes envelop the whole carcass in a coating of propolis. Similarly they cover the shells of snails or tiny lizards which have died in the hive. Any dirt or foreign substance which cannot be removed by the housekeeping bees is kept from contaminating the interior with such a coating of resinous glue. If you place a moth ball in a hive, the insects will quickly cover the offensive object with propolis.

I have saved the two largest enemies of the bee for the last. They are the bear and man. The bear is the hereditary foe of the honeybee. In its quest for sweets, it will wreck the hive and leave the bees destitute. Its great shaggy body is fairly immune to the stings of the aroused insects. They strike for the eyes, ears, nose, and the patches of bare skin where each leg joins the bear's body. If they become entangled in the hair, they work their way down to the skin and sacrifice their lives by plunging their stings into the body of their huge adversary. Unless aid comes to the bees, however, they almost invariably fight a losing battle against the bear.

One of the memorable passages in Gilbert White's *Natural History of Selborne* relates to a feeble-minded village boy who "from a child, showed a strong propensity to bees. They were," says White, "his food, his amusement, his sole object. In winter, he dozed away his time within his father's house, by a fireside, in a kind of torpid state, seldom departing from the chimney corner; but in the summer, he was all alert, in quest of his game in the fields, and on sunny banks.

"Honeybees, bumblebess and wasps were his prey wherever he found them. He had no apprehensions from their stings, but would seize them and at once disarm them of their weapons and suck their bodies for the sake of their honey-bags. Sometimes he would fill his bosom between his shirt and his skin with a number of these captives, and sometimes he would confine them in bottles. He was a very *merops apiaster*, or bee-bird, and very injurious to men that kept bees ; for he would slide into their bee gardens, and, sitting down before the stools, would rap with his fingers on the hives, and so take the bees as they came out. As he ran about, he used to make a humming noise with his lips, resembling the buzzing of bees. This lad was lean and sallow, and of a cadaverous complexion: and, except for his favourite pursuit, in which he was wonderfully adroit, discovered no manner of understanding."

Up until only a few generations ago, beekeepers used to destroy their colonies each fall in order to obtain the honey they had produced. It is a measure of intelligence and advancing civilization that to-day the movable frames, originated by the pioneer American apiculturist, Lorenzo L. Langstroth, permit the beekeeper to take only the surplus honey, leaving his insects intact and with ample supplies to carry them through the months of cold. Except in his carelessness and ignorance, man is no longer one of the enemies of the honeybee.

Even those who shrink from the sight of every bee, remembering painful encounters with pointed stings, must realize (after following through this account of the legion foes this insect must fight for the protection of its life and hard-earned stores) that without its sting the honeybee would long ago have disappeared from the earth. Each worker bee that uses its sting at the same time commits suicide, giving its life for the protection of its colony. In the strangeness of Nature's ways the stinging of the bee is a sacrifice instead of an act of aggression. Anyone who understands the life and problems of the honeybee will not begrudge it this weapon of defence.

Seen beneath the microscope, the sting of the worker bee is far more than a simple piercing lancet. Actually it is formed of two spears sliding and working on each other and operating within the cavity of a guide. Sense organs at the end of this guide tell the bee when it is in contact with the object it intends to sting. The lancet, capable of piercing through the felt of a hat or the leather of a glove, is driven downward by more than twenty different muscles. Once it is inserted, bee-sting venom is forced into the wound. Incidentally, the wound produced by the sting is so small that the skin tends to close over the spot and thus prevent the venom from oozing out.

The bee, once its sting has been driven home, tugs at the anchored lancet, or walks around it, until it breaks off or the end of the abdomen is torn away. Occasionally a bee is able to free the stinger, but such a case is rare. Even after the sting and attached poison sac have been torn free, this fragment of the bee's body continues to function as though it were still part of the living animal. Like a frog's heart, the sac continues to pulsate rhythmically, forcing more and more poison down the shaft of the sting. Under a magnifying glass, such pulsations have been seen continuing for twenty minutes after the sting and the sac have been torn from the body of the bee.

Oftentimes, when you disturb bees, you will see them elevate their abdomens, ready to sting. Tiny droplets collect on the tips of their insect lancets. These droplets are formed of the fluid produced in the two sets of poison glands and mixed in the poison sac. One set of glands produces a fluid which has an acid reaction ; the other a fluid with an alkaline reaction. The two fluids have to be mixed, according to some authorities, before the venom is fully effective. This poison has a sharp, pungent taste and its strong odour quickly excites the bees.

In recent years, another property, of considerable importance to man, has been discovered in this irritating fluid. Its ability to relieve rheumatism, neuritis, and other similar ailments, has received considerable attention by scientists in the U.S.A. and elsewhere, notably by Dr. Bodog F. Beck, of New York City.

The belief that bee venom is good for rheumatism has been held since prehistoric times. It was one of the folk ideas of middle Europe. It remained, however, for scientific research of recent years to give evidence of the soundness of the belief. Several systems of treating patients by bee therapy have been tried. The simplest and earliest procedure was to catch a bee and let it sting the patient. Later, other methods were used. Bees were made to sting through thin membranes and the venom was collected to be injected hypodermically. More recently, a third system has been reported from Europe. Here the venom is mixed into a salve which can be rubbed on muscles and joints affected with rheumatism, neuralgia, sciatica, and lumbago. Crystals of bee poison in the salve are said to make tiny scratches in the skin and thus facilitate absorption of the venom.

8

HOUR OF THE SWARM

DURING the days of late spring, when the liquid gold of the honey flow reaches the hive in an endless stream, a new type of wax creation appears amid the treasure vaults and brood combs of the insect city. It is a pendent cell, about the shape and size of a peanut. Usually it is attached to the side or bottom of the regular comb. In years of plenty, as many as a dozen such cells may be found in a single hive. They are the royal cradles within which are maturing the virgin queens.

When these peanut-shaped cradles appear on the comb, the hour of the swarm—the most dramatic of all the hours in the life of the bee—is near at hand. The old queen, sensing the approach of her new rivals, leads forth thousands of her followers on a daring aerial migration to a destination unknown.

The machinelike routine of the hive is forgotten. Caution, common sense, all the virtues of their everyday lives, are ignored. A holiday spirit sweeps over the insects. They gorge themselves with honey. They seem drunk with joy, delirious at the approach of a great adventure. The frugal, provident, hard-working bees are seemingly caught up in a mad, reckless mood of abandon. They hazard all in one rash gamble with fate. Like ten thousand Ruths following one Naomi, the workers follow the queen to a new home, deserting all they have known and laboured for since birth.

And yet it is not strictly true to say they follow the queen. They cluster where she alights and they encircle her in a vast, living ball of flying insects when she is on the wing. But, in many cases,

79

thousands of the tumultuous throng have already taken to the air before the queen appears. In fact, swarms have been known to leave the hive without a queen. Some higher power, the spirit of the hive, seems to dictate the moment when the swarm begins.

And fate, too, oftentimes decides where the swirling cloud of insects shall alight. One swarm descended on a boy riding a bicycle along a country road, another on a motorcycle going thirty miles an hour on a highway. A third came down on the deck of a steamship several miles from shore. A fourth enveloped the head of a donkey tethered in an open field. And in an old English newspaper, dated July 25, 1813, there is an account of the excitement caused by "a swarm of bees resting themselves on the inside of a lady's umbrella." In West Virginia, a few years ago, a swarm alighted on a freight engine which had paused to take on water at a siding. The bees were still clinging in their exposed position when the train headed away over the mountains.

Once I found a heart-shaped mass of honeycombs hanging from the upper limb of an apple tree, exposed to wind and rain. The swarming bees had alighted in the tree, had been held up by bad weather, and had begun comb building on the spot.

François Huber, a century and a half ago, noted the care with which these insects choose the time of swarming. Bees that are on the point of leaving the hive in a swarm, he says, will delay their departure if a cloud passes over the face of the sun. Usually it is midmorning on a bright sunny day when the hour of the swarm arrives.

Once you have heard the "swarm tone," the peculiar sound of the golden throng when it streams out of the darkness of the hive and swirls upward in a joyous dance in the sunshine, you will never forget it. A time of excitement, of adventure, of dancing and freedom, is at hand. This is the one play day, the only Sunday known in the world of the bees.

It is a hardened beekeeper who can remain calm at such a moment. The excitement is infectious. The queen becomes excited. The workers become excited. Bees, too young to fly, sometimes crawl out of the hive and tumble to the ground. Drones are swept away by the agitation of the crowd and join the swarm. Huber reported that in the tumult before this exodus the temperature within the hive may rise as high as 104 degrees F.

The warmer the weather, as a general rule, the larger the throng that leaves the hive. In some cases, three-fourths of the population of the waxen city takes part in the exodus. New recruits emerge from the interior and join the thousands of insects glinting in the sun as they dart and wheel above the hive. When most of the bees that have attained flying age are in the air, the cloud of insects begins to move away. Sometimes the flight will carry them only half a dozen yards, at other times a mile or more.

Among the many folk-lore beliefs of the past concerning the honeybee are those relating to making swarms alight. The beating of pans, the flashing of light by means of mirrors, the shooting of guns, have at various times, been recommended for making a swarm settle.

The only method of hastening the settling of a swarm that has proved successful is spraying water over the mass of flying insects. Either because the moisture makes them think rain is falling or because it weights down their wings, the insects so treated soon alight.

An English beekeeper reports a curious occurrence which took place some years ago. A swarm from one of his hives alighted in the top of a tall tree. Unable to get to it, the apiarist fired both barrels of a shotgun at the mass, thinking to break it up and send it on to a more easily accessible spot. A few bees fell to the ground, killed by the shot. Soon afterward, the ball of insects broke up and the bees returned to the hive. Among the four or five insects that had been hit and killed by the lead pellets was the queen.

It is the old queen that always leads the first swarm of the season away from the hive. Later on, younger virgin queens, which emerge from the cells stocked with royal jelly, may lead forth other swarms. In years of plentiful food, there may be several of these mass exoduses in which portions of the colony break home ties and leave to establish new insect cities in other locations.

In the annals of our human history the great migrations of peoples have written some of the most dramatic chapters. But nowhere—neither in the wanderings of the Mongols, the travels of the Children of Israel, the trek of the Boers, nor in the westward migration of the Mormons—is there anything more determined or audacious than this quitting the safety of a well-stocked home for the dangers of the unknown.

Once the swarm settles in a great vibrating mass on the limb of a tree or other support, the main frenzy of swarming time has passed. But the insects are still in a holiday mood, at peace with all the world. I have seen a friend of mine lift masses of bees from such a cluster with a tablespoon as though he were ladling grains of oversize wheat. Great handfuls of these creatures, normally so quick to resent undue familiarity, can be scooped up like soft snow. Beekeepers have draped the masses about their heads, have formed long beards of the living insects, without receiving a single sting. A belief of old-time apiarists was that the abdomens of the insects, gorged with honey, were so distended that stinging had become impossible.

If you approach close to the golden mass formed by the tens of thousands of bees, you will see that the insects on the outside of a forming cluster have the tips of their abdomens lifted and their wings fanning. They are sending out a scent signal, a penetrating perfume which leads other bees to the spot. Among the many question marks that punctuate the life of the bee is the mystery of why the swarming insects cluster. What causes them to form their pendent masses remains to be made clear. Usually the queen alights first and the swirling cloud of insects settles down around her. But sometimes thousands of workers alight before the queen joins them. The spirit of the hive, guiding the actions of the colony, seems to dictate the moment of clustering as it does the hour of the swarm. Lost in the midst of the living mass, the queen mother is sheltered and protected by the close-packed bodies of her children.

It is now that the frenzy of the bees abates. They begin to give thought for the morrow ; their normal prudence returns ; their concern once more turns to the labours of their existence. Scout bees dart away in search of a hollow tree, a wall with an entrance in it, some dry and protected spot suitable for the establishment of the new city. The beekeeper who is wise acts before the new home has been chosen. He places the whole mass of clustering insects in an empty hive, where they immediately set up housekeeping with a great show of activity.

If the apiarist hesitates too long, the scouts return and in some mysterious way communicate their find. The bees take to the air in a great swirling ball as large as twenty feet in diameter. Sailing over trees and buildings, the swarm moves off in the direction of its chosen destination.

Here again, you find the early arrivals guiding in the stragglers with olfactory signals. The stream of scent is fanned backward by other bees moving in toward the entrance of the new home. Like a coloured chemical carried down-stream by the current, the scent moves outward into the surrounding air and leads the members of the swarm to a landing. Dr E. F. Philips, for many years in charge of bee research for the U.S. Department of Agriculture, tells of being able to catch the odour given off by the bees when he placed his nose within a couple of inches of the insects.

Streaming into the entrance of the new home, the golden throng disappears from sight. Within, we know, the foundations of a new city of wax soon will be laid with the feverish energy of these active creatures. Cleaning will go on; wax will be created; combs will come into being. The gathering of pollen and nectar; the egg laying of the fertile queen—from now on a prisoner in the darkness of her new home—all the manifold duties of normal routine will soon begin. The great dramatic outburst in the life of the bee colony is over. They have broken old home ties for ever.

When we consider that fact, we perceive that it forms one of the strangest and most dramatic aspects of this strange and dramatic migration. As Maeterlinck so eloquently phrases it, "And even though the beekeeper deposit the hive, in which he has gathered the old queen and her attendant cluster of bees, by the side of the abode they have but this moment quitted, they would seem, be the disaster never so great that shall now have befallen them, to have wholly forgotten the peace and the happy activity that once they had known there, the abundant wealth and the safety that had then been their portion; and all, one by one, and down to the last of them, will perish of hunger and cold around their unfortunate queen rather than return to the home of their birth, whose sweet odour of plenty, the fragrance, indeed, of their own past assiduous labour, reaches them even in their distress."

9

BIRTH OF AN INSECT QUEEN

A LL the difference between a worker bee and a queen, between the tens of thousands of labouring insects and the one mother of the colony—all this difference is produced by a thick white cream, the magic substance known as royal jelly.

If you place a bit of this white substance on the tip of your tongue, you will note its acid taste. I have watched it turn yellow with exposure to the air and have noticed how stubbornly it refuses to mix with water. Many men have felt it, examined it, tasted it, analysed it. Yet its magic properties are not to be discovered by such outward testing. Only in the waxen cradles of the beehive does it reveal its miraculous capacity.

The royal cells, within which this food of the future queens is placed, are attached to the outside or the edge of the comb. During the initial stages of their construction, these cells resemble more than anything else the cap of an acorn. But as they near completion, they assume the shape and size and roughened exterior of a pea-nut. The eggs which are deposited within these larger cells are no different from those laid in the multitude of ordinary worker cradles on the brood comb. The difference is the food with which the larger cells are stocked.

Sometimes, when looking over a field of wheat or other grain, you observe patches where the stalks are taller and greener than those around them. Below these particular plants are areas of greater fertility. Increased nourishment gave the stalks their added height and colour. But the character of the grain they produce is not altered ; the kernels of wheat or oats or rye are the same as those that come from all the other plants within the field.

In the case of the royal jelly also, it is concentrated food that gives added nourishment. But it is amazingly more than that. Royal jelly not only increases the size of the insect but changes its whole character and destiny. It is as though the greener patches of grain, through the nourishment they received alone, produced kernels of a different shape and character from those of the average plant. For, if you take a young grub from a brood-comb cell and feed it royal jelly, it becomes not a worker but a queen.

It was a century and a half ago, in the spring of 1790, that François Huber noted in detail how the bee colony was thus able to produce new queens in an emergency when the old queen was killed and no new royal nymphs were maturing in the larger cells. It is another of Nature's provisions for the welfare of the colony.

But this drama of diet is limited. Ordinarily all grubs receive royal jelly during the first forty-eight hours of their existence. Then, at the end of the second day according to some authorities and at the end of the third day according to others, honey and pollen replace the royal jelly for drone and worker grubs. Only in the case of larvae that have not yet reached this change in diet will the continued feeding of royal jelly prove effective in altering the character of the bee. That is the dividing line beyond which all the royal jelly in the world is unable to change the destiny of the insect. Its character is fixed. The mold is cast.

Up until the second day, at least, the future of a worker grub is thus within the control of the nurse bees. No power on earth, however, can change a drone grub into a queen. Fertilized eggs alone can produce queens. In the hive, at the height of the laying season, there may be thousands of cells holding worker eggs and grubs, any one of which could become a full-maturing, fertile queen if fed on royal jelly. Receiving the regular fare of the brood comb, they emerge as worker insects, smaller in size than the queen and sexually undeveloped.

What gives this magic white cream its ability to change, in both body and character, the developing bee?

The answer lies in the fact that it is more than a rich and concentrated food. It is not, as naturalists thought for generations, merely food that is pre-digested by the workers. Researches have proved that it is a gland extract, the product of the younger worker bees. The glands that produce it are located in the heads of the nurse insects.

The story of gland secretions and their magic effect forms one of the most remarkable chapters in all biology. If you feed a tadpole on thymus-gland secretion, it becomes bigger and darker— but it never turns into a frog. If, instead of the product of the thymus gland, you feed the tadpole the secretion of the adrenal gland, it becomes lighter and lighter instead of darker in hue. Giants and midgets, idiots and geniuses, are produced among humans by the excess or lack of certain gland secretions. And, among the hive dwellers, it is the royal jelly produced by the glands of the workers that makes possible the existence of the queen and the whole complicated fabric of their insect commonwealth.

Royal jelly which I have removed from queen cells has kept without spoiling for days. Tests have shown that this secretion will change its colour and dry out without losing its potency. Professional queen raisers often store up royal jelly and when it is needed, weeks later, moisten it and feed it to the immature queens.

At various stages in the development of these royal bees, I have opened the cells to photograph the changes taking place within. It is possible to remove the grub or nymph from its wax cradle, as Huber and others have done, and by placing it in a glass vial supplied with royal jelly, watch its development from day to day. Through the walls of such transparent cells, research scientists have seen the grubs alter and assume the form of ghostly white nymphs, then darken and harden and become the full-grown insect queens.

During the last days in the royal cell, when the maturing insect is taking on its final form and hue, there is often enacted within the hive a drama of violence and hate. A single queen to a single hive is the law of Nature. The first-born of the royal bees, when several are maturing, hunts down and tears open the cells of her unborn rivals. The first impulse of the emerging queen is to seek and slay the inmates of the other royal cells.

Sometimes, in the hush of an early-summer evening, the beekeeper, walking among the hives, will hear a sound, high and piping, that rises above the low murmur of the workers. It is that strange, stirring, instinctive song of hate uttered by the first-born queen. And sometimes he hears an answer, lower and more muffled—the reply of another queen whose time for emerging has almost come. Thus, answering hate with hate, they give voice to the animosity which is the birthright of these royal sisters.

The first queen to emerge will frequently rush over the brood comb, pushing her way through the busy workers, searching for the cells of her rivals. When one is found, she tears it open, drags out the immature creature she finds within, and thrusts home the scimitar of her sting again and again.

Huber once witnessed a death battle between two queens which had emerged from royal cells at almost precisely the same instant. Like gladiators, they rushed at each other in a fury. Each clamped its jaws on one of its rival's antennae. Then with abdomens curving inward, they drove home their stings over and over again until both bees fell mortally wounded on the comb. Ordinarily, it is said, when two queens are fighting, worker bees surrounding them will move in and separate the combatants if they get into such a position that both are likely to be killed.

Occasionally, when a young queen returns from a mating flight, she enters the wrong hive. Again, two swarms may alight so close that the queens will lock in combat. A struggle between these royal bees is almost invariably a battle to the death. According to Huber, the worker bees, forming a circle of spectators, will grasp a queen and prevent her from moving if her animosity lessens and she attempts to leave the scene of the combat.

These spectator insects apparently have little interest in the outcome of the battle. They are concerned only in seeing one queen demonstrate her supremacy. Within the hive, when a battle between royal sisters takes place, the one that survives is welcomed as queen of the colony.

If a strange queen with an unfamiliar odour enters a hive, the worker bees will attack it at once. Usually, instead of stinging the intruder as they would a strange worker, they ball around her, preventing her from moving. Sometimes such a cluster of living bees will grow until it is as large as an egg. Experienced apiarists have learned that they can save the queen under such circumstances by dropping the ball of bees into a pan of water. Each worker strikes out for herself and the queen can be fished out unharmed.

The almost invariable rule is that only a queen stings a queen. Queens do not sting workers and workers do not sting queens. On one occasion, however, I observed a strange queen attacked and eventually stung to death by the workers of the colony she had invaded. Bees, as someone has remarked, never do anything invariably. Another instance of this truth is the fact that on certain rare occasions two queens have been found in the same hive, both amicably laying eggs on the same brood comb. When this occurs, one of the queens is usually old and her egg-producing days are nearing an end. This is, of course, a surprising exception to the universal rule. One queen to one hive is the symbol and the hub of the honeybees' unity.

Early naturalists confused the sex of this insect and invariably referred to the queen as the king. They thought it directed the activity of the hive in the manner of a human monarch. "The kings," wrote Pliny in his pioneer natural history, "are very fair and goodly to look at; and twice as big as the rest: in their port and manner of march more stately; carrying on their front a white star like a diadem or coronet; far brighter and neater than the common sort. When he marches abroad, the whole army goes forth likewise. About his person he has a certain guard ever attendant; he has his Lictors and officers always in readiness, in token of majesty and princely port. Where the king once settles and takes up his resting-place, there they all pitch their tents and encamp."

Few features of the mystery-filled life of the hive are more strange than the existence of the queen. Her royal battles, her movements within the circle of her close-pressed court, the airy drama of her mating flight, her long imprisonment within the dark corridors of the hive, her steady, machine-like production— day after day, week after week, year after year—of thousands, tens of thousands, hundreds of thousands of eggs, all are carried out in obedience to the dictates of instinct.

When the queen has emerged from her royal cradle and has slain her rivals, she has yet to journey into the outer world on her mating flight. Until this is accomplished, she is no more able to produce fertile eggs than are the worker bees. To build up the thriving, populous city with its legion of workers, its waxen vaults holding stores of honey, its brood chambers with hexagonal cradles filled with the maturing grubs, the virgin queen must quit the dark, familiar corridors of her home and, risking the strangeness of a new element, take wing into a world of blue skies and dazzling sunshine.

10

MATING FLIGHT

I F the hour of the swarm is the outstanding occurrence in the life
of the hive, the mating flight—swirling upward into the blue
of the sky—is the climax of life for the drones. It is the event for
which they were born, the justification of their existence.

All summer long, these burly insects may push their way about
within the crowded hive; all summer they are fed and cared for by
the workers; all summer they subtract from, rather than add to,
the supplies of the golden throng. Larger than the workers and
equipped with great, many-faceted eyes that form a shining crown
covering the sides and almost the whole top of the head, the drones
aid in none of the tasks of the hives. They are incapable of making
wax. They have no pollen baskets for the collecting of floral gold.
They possess no stings to drive off enemies. They gather no
nectar, do none of the fanning or guarding or fighting that protects the stores in the waxen vaults. Yet, just as surely as the
industrious worker, the sluggard drone also plays its part in
Nature's plan. The rendezvous it keeps on some clear and brilliant
summer morning is so vital to the life of the hive that without it
the whole complicated fabric of the insect city would fall asunder.

Few men have ever seen the aerial meeting between drone and
virgin queen. For centuries the sex life of the honeybee was one
of the unsolved riddles of natural science, although it occupied the
attention of all the great pioneers of apiculture. Swammerdam,
in Holland, at first thought that the drones "exhaled an emana-
tion" within the hive and thus fertilized the queens. Réaumur, in

91

France, disproved this by reasoning, and Huber, in Switzerland, by a simple experiment. He separated the drones in a hive and placed them in little tin cans perforated with minute holes. The virgin queen, also a prisoner within the hive, remained unimpregnated. A German scientist of the period held that the queen was able to fertilize herself without the necessity of mating, and an English naturalist arrived at the conclusion, as the result of seeing drones insert their abdomens in brood cells, that after the eggs were laid by the queen they were "bedewed by the males," and thus fertilized.

It was not until June 29, 1788, that the riddle was finally solved. That day, in Pregny, Switzerland, was very warm with the sun shining from a cloudless sky. About eleven o'clock in the morning, Huber and his fellow observer, François Burnens, stationed themselves before the entrance of a hive. The males appeared, took flight, and sported about in the sunshine. Then the young queen, five days out of the royal cell, emerged from the darkness of the interior. She made one short, circling flight and landed—evidently getting her bearings. Then she darted away in rapid circles, rising higher and higher until she was lost to sight. Twenty-seven minutes later, she descended and entered the hive. Huber contracted the entrance so she could not leave again. Soon afterward, he found fertile eggs in the cells. Somewhere on that circling flight into the sky the queen had mated.

Later, Huber constructed a glass box eight feet square and connected it with a hive by means of a transparent tube of the same material. Both drones and a virgin queen entered the enclosure but the space was too small for mating to take place. In recent years, experimenters have observed queens and drones after they have been liberated within large greenhouses and invariably failed to see them mate. The free, open air is always the scene of this winged courtship.

However, such observers have noted a curious fact. The moment a flying queen alighted on the glass roof of the greenhouse, the pursuing drones lost interest in her. A thousand times, within the close-packed corridors of the hive, the males pass by the virgin queen without paying the least attention to her. I have seen a drone push its way almost into the circle of workers that formed the court of a queen and show no sign of unusual interest. It is only the flying insect, the young queen circling on her mating flight, that attracts their attention and leads them to pursuit.

On occasions, a pursuing male will overtake the queen only a few feet from the ground instead of high in the air. It has been on such occasions that fortunate observers have been able to witness the event which puzzled scientists for so long and to fill in a blank page in our knowledge concerning the life of the honeybee.

The mating takes place in the brightest and hottest part of the day. It never occurs in cloudy or rainy weather. Always the young queen is between five and seven days old when she leave the hive. As she begins her upward spiral, the great eyes of the drones catch sight of her darting form. A score or more will set out in pursuit, trailing behind with wings blurring at top speed in their effort to overtake the fleeing female. Thus they may mount upward, higher and higher, until they disappear from sight.

Somewhere, at the climax of this aerial pursuit, one of the train of suitors, a drone stronger or fleeter of wing than the rest, overtakes the queen. In this manner, it has been suggested, Nature insures the strength of the strain within the hive. The upward rush of queen and drones is, in effect, a weeding-out process. Only the strong attain the fair among the honeybees.

For this favoured one, however, the attainment of its goal is the end' as well as the climax of its life. For it, success and death are close companions. Those who have witnessed the actual mating, when it has occurred near the ground, give us an insight into what happens in the sky. On overtaking the queen, the drone circles swiftly, then grasps her face to face. For some distance, the embracing insects flying in a position almost vertical to the ground. Then they both tumble to the earth or the queen pulls herself free in mid-air. In either case, the whole end of the drone's abdomen is torn away. Fatally injured, it dies within a short time.

Sometimes this tragedy, in which the death of the drone brings new life to the hive, is enacted within the space of a few minutes. Again, the mating flight may last half an hour or longer. When the queen returns to the hive, with the white generative organs of the male trailing behind, the workers become greatly excited. They crowd about and assist the queen in removing these evidences of success in the mating. Outside the hive, a crowd of drones which have followed the queen back to the landing stage may circle about for as many as several hours, as though awaiting the reappearance of the female.

Sometimes queens do emerge again into the outer air after a mating flight. A century and a half ago, Huber reported that queens may mate more than once; but up until 1904, most bee authorities held that a single mating flight is all that any queen ever makes. More recent research has proved that the painstaking Swiss "historian of the bees" was right.

Among the drones who take up the pursuit of the queen, there may be representatives from many hives. In this way, Nature avoids the dangers of inbreeding. But, for the modern scientist seeking to develop new and better strains, the haphazard selecting of a mate in the sky presents many problems. In the past, innumerable attempts to choose the mate of the queen—in an effort to produce better bees by selective breeding, as is done with cattle and horses—have met with failure. Larger and larger enclosures were used, within which selected drones and queens were released. But, in every case, mating failed to take place.

In 1883, a beekeeper in Canada, named D. A. Jones, used a novel method for controlling the breeding of his insects. On three remote islands he placed apiaries, containing Cyprian, Syrian, and Palestine bees. Each island was named after the kind of bee it supported. Unable to interbreed, the colonies on the different islands produced only offspring of their own strain. However, the expense involved in maintaining the isolated apiaries made the venture unprofitable.

The greatest success in selective breeding through isolation was attained in Switzerland. Here, hives were placed in high valleys where surrounding natural barriers kept out other bees and where only queens and drones of the single strain could mate. The labour involved and the fact that birds, storms, and preying insects often destroyed the queens and their pursuing drones during mating flights, resulted in the abandonment of the scheme.

Not through isolation but through laboratory research has science found a path to selective breeding among the bees. One of the greatest advances in apiculture in recent history was announced in the mid-thirties of the present century. In a laboratory at Alfred University, at Alfred, New York, Dr L. R. Watson succeeded in fertilizing a queen artificially. In a delicate operation, made beneath a microscope, he transferred the male cells from a drone to the queen. In this operation, as well as in natural mating, the drone loses his life. But the queen is unharmed by the process of artificial insemination and her life in the hive henceforth is entirely normal.

Other scientists beside Dr Watson are using the technique which he developed. Department of Agriculture research workers, in Washington, D. C., were quick to see the possibilities of the method. Drones and queens, for the first time, could be selected for desired characteristics and mated by the laboratory operation. Different types of bees could be crossed as desired to develop new qualities—gentler strains; bees that could carry more honey, fly farther in search of nectar, live longer. A whole new realm of possibilities has been opened up by the success of the Alfred scientist. Experiments along this line had been made previously, but they never attained complete success. For the first time in the thousands·of years that man and bees have been working together, man has found a way to govern the evolution of his insects.

But whether the queen returns to the hive after a natural mating flight in the sky or from the miniature operating table formed by the stage of a high-powered microscope where artificial insemination takes place, her actions from then on are the same. Within forty-eight hours, she begins laying eggs in the brood cells which are cleaned and prepared by the worker bees. Each egg is comma-shaped and whitish-grey. It is attached to the base of the cell with a secretion produced by the queen. As the egg is laid, the destiny of the bee which will hatch from it is determined.

If the bee is to be a worker, the egg is fertilized with male cells which are kept in a sac resembling a drawstring pouch, within the body of the queen. At the time of mating this pouch is filled with millions of spermatozoa, sufficient male cells to last during the lifetime of the queen. An amazing feature of this procedure is the fact that whereas human sperm cells have a life of but twelve days at the longest, the cells in the pouch of the queen honeybee retain their vitality for years. The British entomologist F. R. Cheshire calculated that during the mating flight the queen bee receives upwards of 4,000,000 sperm cells. During her lifetime, according to this same authority, a vigorous queen may lay as many as 1,500,000 eggs.

At the height of the laying period, a queen will deposit from four to six eggs a minute. She is capable of producing 5,000 a day, although the peak is usually between 1,500 and 2,000. Sometimes, a queen will lay more than her own weight in eggs during a single

THIRTY THOUSAND BEES clustering together in a swarm. Such masses of living insects have alighted on trains, on donkeys, on umbrellas, on ships miles from shore, even on cyclists pedalling down country lanes.

SCENT SIGNALS attract swarming bees to the cluster. As the insects settle, those on the outside of the mass open scent glands and, by means of fanning wings, send out a stream of odour, guiding other bees to the spot.

EGG LAYER for the colony is the honeybee queen. During her active years, she may deposit more than 1,000,000 eggs in the cells prepared by workers. Sometimes she lays more than her weight in eggs in a single day.

INVASION. Young queens returning from their mating flights sometimes enter
the wrong hive. Almost invariably the two queens battle to the death. In the two
pictures on this and the following page, the camera has caught the rare occurrence

[over

of workers attacking the invading queen. Note that the queen of the invaded hive is apparently an onlooker in this remarkable photographic sequence. A moment after this picture was snapped, the attacking queen was stung to death by the workers.

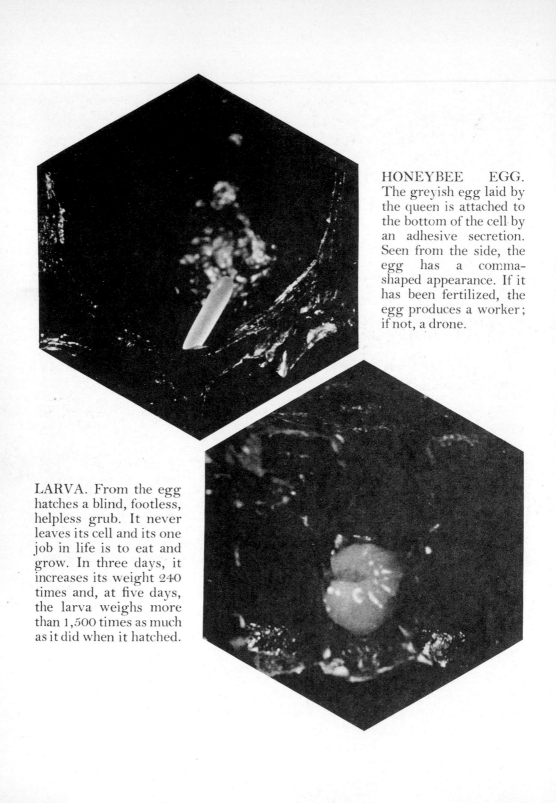

HONEYBEE EGG. The greyish egg laid by the queen is attached to the bottom of the cell by an adhesive secretion. Seen from the side, the egg has a comma-shaped appearance. If it has been fertilized, the egg produces a worker; if not, a drone.

LARVA. From the egg hatches a blind, footless, helpless grub. It never leaves its cell and its one job in life is to eat and grow. In three days, it increases its weight 240 times and, at five days, the larva weighs more than 1,500 times as much as it did when it hatched.

THIRTEEN HUNDRED MEALS A DAY are often fed the grubs by the nurse
bees. During the final day before the larvae begin spinning their cocoons and
cease eating, nurse bees may be feeding them twenty per cent of the time.

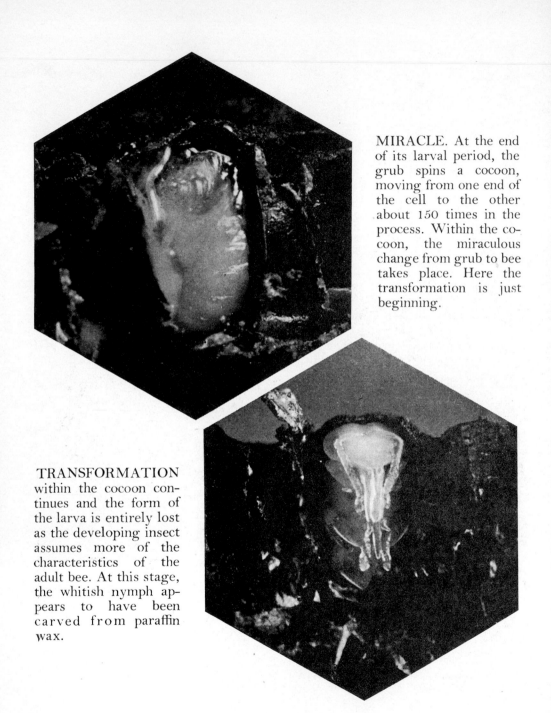

MIRACLE. At the end of its larval period, the grub spins a cocoon, moving from one end of the cell to the other about 150 times in the process. Within the cocoon, the miraculous change from grub to bee takes place. Here the transformation is just beginning.

TRANSFORMATION within the cocoon continues and the form of the larva is entirely lost as the developing insect assumes more of the characteristics of the adult bee. At this stage, the whitish nymph appears to have been carved from paraffin wax.

NYMPH. The transformation from grub to adult bee almost complete, the milk-white nymph lies in its cradle of wax covered with a porous capping.

BIRTHDAY in a beehive. The transformation from larva to adult completed, the bee pushes or bites the porous cap from the top of its cell and prepares to emerge. In large hives, 1,000 bees a day often emerge in this way.

CLIMAX in the development of the young bee comes when, with wings folded tightly along its body and antennae stretched out before it, it pulls itself quickly from the brood cell and enters the busy world of the hive.

NEWBORN bees at first engage in tasks within the hive. They are about fifteen days old before they go afield. The duties performed by the individual bee are determined by the development of glands within its body.

LIVING FAN. Millions of years before man appeared on earth, bees were air-conditioning their homes with fanning wings. This remarkable picture shows a worker regulating the temperature of the hive by circulating fresh air through the interior.

COMMUNICATION   The extended mouthparts of a worker can be clearly seen as it receives nectar and information from another worker.

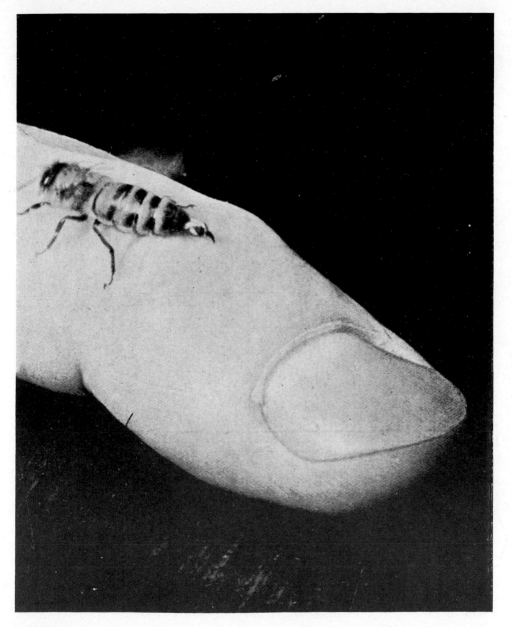

SUICIDE OF A BEE. This remarkable picture shows a stinging bee in the act of pulling away the whole end of its abdomen, after driving its barbed sting into the flesh of the victim. Almost always, for the bee, to sting is to die.

THE THRESHOLD OF THE HIVE is a scene of intense activity. Foraging bees come and go. Guards watch for enemies. Workers, with blurring wings, cool the interior. The bustle and activity suggests market day in a country town.

day. As she moves about from one cell to the next, she follows a circular path, each revolution of which adds to the diameter of the brood area. Throughout these labours, the queen is attended by the court bees, a circle of workers which face toward her and continually rub her with their antennae. After as long as half an hour of steady laying, the queen mother pauses for rest. This lasts for perhaps five minutes before work is resumed. During this rest period, the workers press close and feed the queen what is thought to be that concentrated food, royal jelly.

A startling change comes over the queen if her antennae are damaged or removed while she is laying her eggs. Huber tells of one instance in which he amputated both antennae from the head of a laying queen. Thereafter she appeared unable to guide herself within the crowded interior of the observation hive. She wandered aimlessly about, turning this way and that. Instead of her usual care in placing her eggs in the cells, she dropped them without regard to where they fell. The workers of her court were unable to feed her because she seemed to have lost her ability to locate their mouths when they approached. The senses located in the antennae of the queen are apparently as vital to her in the darkness of the hive as they are to the worker bees in the sunshine of the open fields.

Sometimes a queen is held up by storms or periods of prolonged bad weather when she is ready to make her mating flight. In such a case, she may lose all desire to leave the hive. She begins laying eggs—unfertile eggs because she had no male cells with which to fertilize them. The pouch, which normally is filled with millions of spermatozoa, is empty. Only drones emerge from the cells of the brood comb, and the hive is doomed.

Similarly, worker bees, in times when the queen is lost or killed and no new queens can be produced, will begin laying eggs. This desperate attempt to keep the colony alive is always a failure.

The workers, sexually undeveloped and incapable of mating, can produce none but unfertilized eggs. The burden of the drones increases, while the number of workers to support them grows less, and eventually the whole unfortunate colony, as though swept by some slow-working blight, disintegrates and disappears.

The discovery that workers are capable of laying eggs was verified by one of the most painstaking and exhausting pieces of investigation in the history of honeybee research. Huber, in 1788, had found eggs in the brood cells of a hive which had been deprived for some time of its queen. Another eminent scientist of the day suggested they were laid by a "little queen," a female which had escaped notice because it was no larger than the workers. There was only one way to refute the contention and that was to examine every one of the tens of thousands of insects that made up the colony. Huber's ever-faithful servant, Burnens, volunteered to discharge the staggering task.

For eleven days, with only fleeting periods of relaxation to rest his eyes, this student of the bees continued his work. One at a time, he examined the bodies of the insects under a microscope. Every one had the characteristics of either a worker or a drone. Not one showed the easily distinguished features of the queen. One final step in the researches eliminated all possibility that the eggs had been laid by a "little queen" which had escaped before the hive had been closed for the examination. All the workers, as they were examined, were placed in a glass cage containing brood comb and honeycomb. Soon eggs began to appear in the brood cells. They could have been laid only by the prisoners, only by the insects which had been identified—each and every one of them—as worker bees.

It is the greyish, comma-shaped eggs of the fertilized queen alone, however, that insure the continued existence of the golden throng. The nuptial flight of a young queen is the foundation of life in the hive from which a swarm has departed. Her eggs, filling the cells of the brood chamber, will keep an army of nurse bees active day and night, and from them will come the constantly replenished population of the hive—the workers and drones and future queens of this teeming insect city.

11

NURSERIES

THE story of my glass-walled hive, or of any other habitation of the bees, is a record of violent contrasts: the brilliant sunshine of the open fields and the close-packed darkness of the hive, the endless labours of the worker bees and the happy-go-lucky lives of the drones, the far-flying activity of the nectar gatherers and the sedentary, indoor existence of the egg-laying queen mother of the colony.

When her labours begin in the early spring, the drama enacted on the stage of my observation hive takes on added interest. There is the activity of the royal court, attending and feeding the queen, moving like a dull-golden elliptical brooch across the brood comb as the egg layer of the colony advances from cell to cell. There is the thorough work of the cleaners, workers that prepare the cells in the path of the advancing queen. There is the harried labour of the nurse bees, moving from grub to grub. And, finally, there are the emerging, newborn workers and drones, shining and downy, appearing to the casual eye to have been turned out of glistening metal, all from an identical mould.

During the height of the summer season, in a large hive, 1,500 new bees may bite their way from the brood-comb cells in the course of a single day. Out in the fields, an equal number of worn-out workers may have perished during the same twenty-four hours—reaching the end of their supply of energy, unable to lift the last load of nectar, exhausted by their weeks of concentrated toil.

In the early days of egg laying, at a time when spring flowers are opening and the first replenishing pollen and nectar are coming into the hive, none but the fertilized eggs of worker bees are deposited by the queen. She will pass by the larger drone cells if she meets them in her slow, spiral course over the surface of the brood comb. Later, after the colony has been supplied with thousands of active workers, it is ready to support the luxury of non-productive drones. The present must be cared for before the future can be considered.

If you glance through the glass wall of an observation hive at the cells in the wake of the advancing queen, you can see near the bottom of each a one-sixteenth-inch-long, greyish, comma-shaped egg. Always it is attached by the "tail of the comma." The enlarged end, representing the head of the larva which will hatch from it, is invariably uppermost. Enclosing the egg is a thin, tough membrane called chorin. Within this chorin envelope is the nucleus, the surrounding protoplasm, and the stored-up food, or yolk, of the egg.

For three days, the tiny embryo within its chorion shell develops and changes. At the end of that time, it breaks through the membrane and emerges in the form of a larva. Pure white, blind, footless, helpless, it is a simple organism consisting almost entirely of stomach. It looks a great deal like one of those beetle larvae or grubworms you spade up in the garden in early spring. It has no antennae. It has no wings. It has no legs. It has no eyes. The fact that it is protected within its cell and is fed by nurse bees enables it to survive with the simplest sort of bodily equipment. Its one goal in life is to eat and grow.

It does both to an astonishing degree. Bruce Lineburg, of the U.S. Department of Agriculture, has made some fascinating observations on the work of the nurse bees which you see caring for the grubs within the brood cells. On the average, they feed each larva 1,300 *meals a day!*

You see them hurrying from cell to cell, pushing their heads far down into the wax cradles to feed the helpless creatures within. During the days which intervene between the appearance of the larva from the egg and the time it spins its cocoon and begins its metamorphosis into the adult bee, the nurses may feed it as many as 10,000 times. As the grub grows larger, the frequency of the visits increases. During the last day of its existence in grub form, a larva is being fed nearly twenty per cent of the time!

As a result of this almost continuous feeding, the grub increases its size and weight at an almost incredible rate. It is more than 240 times its original size at the end of three days and more than 1,570 times when it spins its cocoon on the fifth day. The rapidity with which it has grown has necessitated changing its skin, or moulting, about once every twenty-four hours. For the grub, like the adult bee, is encased in a shell of chitin, the armour material of all insects. However, this shell is very thin for the larva, far thicker for the adult.

The food which has been served to the cradles in this remarkable building-up process within the nurseries of the hive has varied as the size of the grubs increased. As we have seen, all the larvae, whether drones or workers, receive the same fare—royal jelly—at first. Frequently, you can glimpse this white substance at the very bottom of the cell with the day-old grub, suggesting a stubby quarter-moon, curled up in the middle of its supply of food. After the passing of the second day, however, honey and pollen replace the royal jelly as the diet of the workers and drones.

Outside the brood comb, special cells are set aside as "pantry shelves" for the storing of food used in feeding the larvae. Pollen is packed so tightly into such cells that it forms solid "cartridges" or six-sided pills which may be removed intact. In examining such pollen cartridges, I have been interested to note lines of varying colours running through them like the layers of a cake. Such strata were produced by pollen obtained from different kinds of flowers.

While the nurse bees have been caring for the grubs, the queen has been engaged in an interesting procedure. As has previously been related, her egg laying is accomplished by moving in concentric circles. Thus the eggs at the centre of the brood comb hatch first; those on the circumference, last. Sometimes eggs which have been laid in cells never hatch. The queen will push her way among the busy nurses and hunt out these unproductive cells depositing another egg beside the first. When the inner cradles have produced their adult bees and are empty, the queen mother of the hive returns to the spot where she began and starts her circling journey of egg laying all over again. In large hives, during the most productive part of the year, 40,000 cells may contain developing bees at the same time.

The heat produced by the activity of the cluster of nurse bees is said to maintain a temperature approximately that of our blood heat in and around the brood comb. If the temperature rises too high, the fanning of wings produces an air current which cools the interior of the hive. It has been calculated that each new bee that reaches maturity has cost the hive the equivalent, in food and energy expenditure, of one cellful of honey.

On the sixth day after it has emerged from the egg, the worker-bee larva begins spinning its cocoon. In drones, this occurs half a day later. The silk glands are located in the mouth of the larva. They are used only at this time and disappear during the transformation into the adult insect. In creating the tough, thin little envelope within which the metamorphosis takes place, the grub moves approximately 150 times from one end of its wax cell to the other. When the cocoon is finished, the larva rests. Meanwhile, the cell in which it is lying has been capped over with porous wax by the attendant nurses.

Now comes that wonderful change in which the whole character and form of the creature alters. Huber and other experimenters who have watched bee grubs in tiny glass vials have seen them spin their cocoons. Just what happens within the shell of silk is so complex that it can be described most satisfactorily in terms of external changes. The tiny head of the larva expands to the size and shape of the head of the adult bee; the sacklike body of the grub changes form and assumes the three divisions of the mature insect; the nervous system alters and the eyes, antennae, legs, and wings take shape. All this occurs during the days the immature bee spends within its silken cocoon. This period is twelve days for the worker and fourteen and a half for the drone.

If you remove one of these cocoons and cut open the outer envelope, the creature you find inside appears entirely lifeless. Yet within its slowly altering body, internal changes are consuming so much energy that half the weight of the bee grub is lost during the metamorphosis.

I have opened cells at various stages to observe the maturing creature within. As the nymphs develop inside the cocoons, they appear carved of pure white or paraffin wax. Only during the later stages of their transformation do they begin to darken and take on the colour of the adult. The compound eyes, for instance, are white at first. Then they assume a pinkish cast which turns to brown and finally to black. It is during these later stages, too, that the hard chitin shell forms over the body of the bee. This shell is the skeleton the insect will keep the rest of its life.

One of the most dramatic changes of all occurs near the end of its imprisonment in the cocoon. From hollow, budlike growths on the side of the thorax or middle body of the forming insect, come the legs and wings. Blood pressure forces them out, after which the vital fluid flows back to the body cavity of the nymph. Its time for entering the crowded, busy life of the hive is close at hand.

Your first sight of the newborn bee is its face appearing at an opening made in the wax capping. The nymph always faces the capped end of the cell when lying within its cocoon. Biting its way through the silken envelope which surrounds it, the young bee reaches the underside of the wax cap and pushes or bites its way to freedom. Frequently, I have seen nurse bees apparently aiding the exit of these newborn insects. Little irregular pieces of wax, and sometimes perfect disks, will be found forming small windows at the bottom of the hive after a large number of bees have emerged from the brood cells.

As you watch the cap of a cell from which a young bee is about to emerge, you see one side of the circumference begin to split and lift, or you notice irregular openings appear in the plate of wax. Eventually, in the circular opening of the brood cell there appears the black, heart-shaped face of the emerging bee. If this occurs in an observation hive, light, for the first time, is striking the great compound eyes. The redolent odour of the hive, soon to become so familiar, is striking, for the first time, the sense plates of the antennae.

Quickly the young bee pulls itself through the circular opening, its wings folded tightly along its body. Its antennae stretch out in front of it and move about. It walks across the brood comb among the hurrying nurses and enters the world for which it was created, a world which it can never abandon without embracing death. For the honeybee is incapable of caring for itself alone. It needs the help of its fellow workers to perform the tasks of the insect city, to gather and store honey, and make possible the continued life of the whole. So rapid is the honeybee's assimilation of food and so small is its reserve supply that it dies in a few hours if its source of nourishment is cut off. The thousands of bees in a hive, like the red corpuscles of the blood stream, must return regularly to the crowded corridors of wax just as the corpuscles do to the heart and lungs. Bees spread to every part of the neighbouring territory ; but they continually return again to the heart of their activity, the hive.

The length of time required for a young bee to reach maturity varies according to its caste. From egg to adult for the queen requires only sixteen days. For the worker bee, the elapsed time is twenty-one days ; for the drone, twenty-four. The speed of development, thus, is in direct proportion to the usefulness of the insect. The queen, most vital of all to the welfare of the insect commonwealth, is produced in the shortest space of time ; the worker, next in value, in the second shortest space of time ; and the drone, needed only on rare occasions, in the longest elapsed time of all.

Years ago, watchers of the hive hit upon a simple method of discovering just what the newborn bee does during the first days after it appears from its waxen cradle. They placed a small amount of brood comb containing golden Italian bees in a hive housing black bees. The emerging, yellow insects could be seen easily and their activity noted through the glass walls of the observation hive. Through such studies, and other researches, the early life of the adult has become familiar.

For a day or so, these newborn bees remain on the comb, moving about but little. Then, after the second day, they assume their first duty, feeding the older larvae with honey and pollen. This continues until the sixth day, when the young workers begin supplying royal jelly to the grubs. These early duties keep the workers confined within the bee city. It is not until they are about fifteen days old that they enter a new element, the air. At first they try out their wings in short excursions or play flights. Only a few feet from the entrance of the hive, they circle about in the bright sunshine. Sometimes so many of these whirling fledglings are circling in the sun that they give the impression that a swarm is starting.

Even after these early flights abroad, the young workers continue to labour within the hive for more than a week longer. They receive the nectar brought in by foraging bees, they produce wax for comb building, they circulate air through the interior with fanning wings, and they guard the entrance of the hive. The final stage of their life story sees the workers abandoning their hive duties and taking to the open fields. From then on, they spend their lives foraging for nectar and pollen; propolis, or bee glue; and water. During the height of the brood period, worker bees can be seen clustering along the edge of shallow ponds or pools collecting water to carry back to the hive. On the Isle of Man, country people used to believe that all bees go down to the sea twice a day to drink. Another odd belief once held about bees and water was that the drones were born to be water carriers for the hive.

In recent years, the researches of G. A. Rösch, in Germany, have shown that workers follow a definite sequence of activity, governed by the clockwork of developing glands. "Every bee, of a given age," declares this European scientist, "performs the same specific functions." The successive hatchings in the brood comb provide workers of all ages within the flourishing colony, bees equipped for all the varied tasks required. According to Rösch, the life of the worker is divided into three stages. In the earliest period, the glands which produce the royal jelly are most active. It is then that the bees are nurses, feeding and caring for the brood. The second stage begins with the first flight from the hive. In the period between these initial excursions on the wing and the beginning of nectar hunting, the wax-secreting glands are especially active and the bees are most often engaged in comb building. The final stage of the worker's life carries it continually afield. It is while engaged in these tasks that it comes to the end of its days.

As long ago as 1855, another European scientist reported that when he dipped a stick in honey and offered it to young workers taken from a hive they ignored the sweet. From this experiment, he concluded that the young bees, during their royal-jelly and wax-producing periods, lacked the impulse to gather honey. That comes later, in the third stage of the honeybee's life cycle.

Within the nurseries of the hive, the activity begins to slow down after the peak of summer is passed. The queen lays fewer eggs. Her one purpose in life—to produce new workers and drones and queens—has kept her labouring throughout the summer. Newborn bees continue to appear from their waxen cradles. But the feverish intensity of earlier weeks is passing. In the dusty, quiet days of early autumn, the colony is chiefly concerned with preparations for the coming winter.

LAWS OF THE CITY

A CROSS a quarter of a mile of sea moor, two swallows on swift grey wings once followed me, circling and twittering, often flashing past less than a dozen feet away. When I advanced, they advanced with me. When I stopped, they circled about, waiting for me to move. Fascinated by their friendly interest, I progressed slowly across the moor and out upon a stretch of barren sand. My aerial companions accompanied me to the very edge of the sand. Then they darted off in wide erratic circles over the vegetation behind.

In a flash, I realized that their interest in me had been only incidental. They had hovered close and kept me company only so long as my progress through the moor grass had sent gauzy-winged flies and other insect titbits fluttering aloft from the vegetation. They had followed me as sea birds follow a steamer, interested primarily in the food that floats in its wake.

So often, when we try to translate the obvious *what* in the behaviour of wild creatures into the obscure *why*—when we leap from the observed action to the supposed motive—we plunge into the pitfalls of error, misjudging causes of the effects we see.

I remember another instance of the kind which occurred beside a thin path which wound between dense vegetation on the border of a swamp. Amid this green tangle, one weed, taller than the rest, caught my eye. Half a dozen black ants were moving slowly among clustering green masses of aphides. So fond are the ants of the sweet honeydew these plant lice exude that they often stand guard and protect the defenceless sap drinkers from their many insect foes.

I tapped the plant with a forefinger. Instantly, the black ants ran this way and that, like faithless shepherds deserting their flocks. A moment later, however, when I moved a leaf, the better to see the actions of the cowardly guards, they rushed upon my finger with open jaws, attacking me fearlessly. On the instant, I regretted the sorry injustice I had done them. My snap judgment had blinded me to the obvious truth. The inefficient eyesight of the ants enabled them to see but dimly. The seeming cowardice of the guards was in reality an exhibition of courage ; their apparent terror-stricken flight, a fearless, near-sighted search for an unseen foe.

In looking through the windows of my hive upon the activity of the bees within, I not infrequently remember the ants and the swallows. Seeking to reason out the purpose of some mystifying action, I recall the ease of error, the difficulty of proof, in the mental jump from effect back to cause.

Half an hour before these words were written, I noticed one of my bees moving feebly about on the floor of the hive. Another worker circled about it a dozen times, went over it from head to tail, seemed to massage it, cleaned each individual leg, touched it a hundred times with its antennae. Again and again, it walked away only to return once more to its strange activity.

For ten minutes, while other bees bustled past, the singular performance went on. In the end, the insect whose activity I had been watching flipped its wings, cleaned its antennae, brushed the dust—so to speak—from its hands, and pushed its way into the throng on the comb above. The ailing worker still moved feebly in aimless circles on the floor of the hive.

What had been taking place within a few inches of my eyes? I could only guess at the exact meaning of what I had seen, recalling the remark of a scientist friend: "If we could only become bees, even for an hour," he had said, "we would learn more about their lives and motives than centuries of human observation will teach us."

As we peer across the boundaries of the bee's world, we all see and feel and hear with human senses. We consider and weigh events with human brains. And, unconsciously, we think of the insects as meeting the problems of their existence with our senses and our outlook.

Instead, virtually all of the actions of the bees are instinctive and unpremeditated. The laws of the hive are written in protoplasm. They are the heritage of millions of years. Like physicists of the laboratory who photograph atom tracks without seeing the atoms, we who watch the bees see evidences of these invisible laws to which queen and worker alike are subject. For want of a more precise term, we refer to the guiding influence of these natural laws as "the spirit of the hive."

It is the spirit of the hive that dictates the hour of the swarm and the massacre of the males. It is the spirit of the hive that produces the mystifying actions of the bees. As the riddle of life transforms a million tiny cells into an animal entity, so the spirit of the hive knits the tens of thousands of individual bees into the living unit of the colony.

As has been related in another chapter, the swarm sometimes seems to start without a leader. The hub about which life in the hive revolves, the queen, does not always lead in the exodus. Sometimes it is well under way before she appears and in a few instances honeybees have been known to swarm without the queen. Again, when the swarming insects settle in a living golden mass upon some limb or other support, the queen is not always the first to land. She is the centre of activity but not the dictator of the golden throng. The queen is the symbol of unity rather than the seat of authority in the colony, the flag on the masthead rather than the rudder of the ship. The invisible laws of the hive which hold the bees together govern her actions as well as those of the least of the workers.

Yet, when disaster befalls a colony, the spirit of the hive dictates that the workers give their lives to save the queen mother. She is the only member of the colony capable of laying the eggs upon which the future of the hive depends. As the number of attendant bees around her decreases in misfortune, they continue to feed her while one by one they themselves die of starvation. In the hive the life of the egg-laying queen mother is most sacred of all.

In the normal course of life, most of the bees come to their end in the open fields. With wings frayed from the winds and from contact with tens of thousands of leaves and petals, the summer workers reach the limit of their strength and expire, seeking to lift one last load of nectar. Their tenacity and singleness of purpose recall the Pilgrim in *Pilgrim's Progress*. "This I have resolved upon," he said, "to wit, to run when I can, to go when I cannot run, and to creep when I cannot go !"

Bees that die within the hive are carried outside by the workers. Yet, seemingly, this is a rare occurrence. As many observers have reported, dying bees will use their remaining strength to creep beyond the threshold or the landing stage. A law of the insect city apparently leads the exhausted bees to leave the interior and so save their fellow workers the task of removing their bodies. The queen seems to be guided by the same instinct, leaving the hive when her end is near.

For cleanliness is one of the unwritten laws of the insect city. It is inherent in the bees. Every fragment of refuse is carried away. If small amounts of some foreign dust are blown among the combs, the observer will see the insects falling to work at once, clearing away every particle of the unwanted substance. As we have seen, when snails and other small creatures die within the hive, the law of cleanliness dictates that they be covered with an airtight mummy case of sanitary and resinous bee glue.

Anyone who watches day after day the infinitely varied activity of the bees finds an increasing source of amazement in the manner in which each insect, like a cog in a smooth-functioning machine, plays its part. Some bees, apparently just the right number, are standing guard at the door; others, apparently just the number required for the task, are air-conditioning the interior ; others are feeding the grubs, cleaning the hive, producing royal jelly for the younger larvae, storing honey, gathering pollen. And so, under the varying conditions of the year, each active worker of the hive goes about her appointed tasks.

Appointed tasks—appointed by whom? In olden days, it was accepted that the queen, or the king as she was then called, directed all the activity of the colony, issued orders, apportioned work, functioned in the manner of a general deploying an army. This, of course, has been proved a fallacy. The queen has her appointed tasks just as the workers do. She, too, is but servant to the spirit of the colony.

By the clever experiments of von Frisch, we have recently learned how the activity beyond the portals of the hive is regulated—how bees use their effort to the best advantage, how they gain knowledge of flowers with the richest supply of nectar, how the number of workers in a given field is balanced to the requirements of the nectar supply. His researches have helped explain how the spirit of the hive functions abroad.

Other studies, particularly those of Rösch, have given a hint as to how the spirit of the hive governs the activity within. They show, as we have seen, that various glands in the bodies of the bees develop in succession and that their development turns the individual worker bee from one task to another. Thus, developing glands, scent and taste, changing temperatures and shifting seasons, play their part as the laws of the city are automatically put into operation for the good of the whole.

There is an old story about a time when all the people of the earth gathered together to set up a single united shout and attract the attention of Mars. The moment arrived. Each took a deep breath. And then nobody uttered a sound except one old man who was deaf. Everybody else was listening to hear what the tremendous halloo would sound like!

With the bees, on the contrary, the union that is their strength is instinctive. The laws of their insect city are handed on from generation to generation. A bee springs full-fledged from the cell in which it matures. Within its body are the sealed orders which will be revealed in regular succession as its life progresses. The spirit of the hive, which orders its days and nights—in the main—holds it as though in the grip of centrifugal force to the path of its co-operative destiny.

It was Victor Hugo, I think, who once remarked that the most interesting thing in the world is something occurring on the other side of a high wall. In our study of the bees, we have substituted glass for wood, we have provided ourselves with windows that reveal the interior of the waxen city, we have seen events that once occurred only behind a screening wall of wood and darkness. Yet, through it all, we realize that a higher wall rises before us, the invisible wall behind which all the natural laws we call the spirit of the hive are functioning.

Scientists who study the bee—chemists who analyze the content of royal jelly, microscopists who attempt to count the sperm cells in the pouch of the fertilized queen, physicists who measure the stresses of honeycomb, all reveal the physical characteristics of the bee and its surroundings. But beyond this lies that intangible, mystical force, the spirit of the hive, running through all the activity of the golden throng ; ordering the lives of the insects ; moulding them into the compact, unified, efficient commonwealth we know.

13

THE BEE IN LORE AND LEGEND

BEES are skilled astronomers. They can predict rain. They were created from rays of light. They suck their young, completely formed, from flowers. Honey is created in the air when the stars rise and a rainbow rests on the earth. At exactly midnight on Christmas Eve bees always hum hymns to celebrate the birth of Christ. And, when they die, bees—alone among all the insects—go to heaven.

Such are some of the strange beliefs about these creatures which have been so long and so closely associated with man.

In the sacred books of many lands, ranging from the *Rig-Veda*, written in Sanskrit between 2000 and 3000 B.C., to *The Book of Mormon*, first printed in 1830, the bee has had a significant place. The Koran contains a whole chapter entitled "The Bee"; and according to the teachings of Mohammed, this insect is the only creature ever directly spoken to by the Lord. Again and again, Hebrew writers of the Bible mention the bee and its works and the sweetness of the honey it makes. Christianity, in fact, aided the spread of beekeeping. For, in addition to valuing the insect as a provider of honey, early church fathers extolled its virtues: chastity, frugality, and industry. Our American names of spelling bee, husking bee, quilting bee, come from both the social and industrious nature of the hive dwellers.

According to *The Book of Mormon*, deseret, the honeybee, was carried by the Jaredites when they journeyed into the valley of Nimrod. The word *deseret* has mystic significance in the teachings of this religion. When the state of Utah was admitted to the Union in 1896, Deseret was the name first proposed. To-day the great seal of this state has at its centre a beehive surrounded by flowers and overhead the word "Industry." Colloquially, Utah is known as "The Beehive State."

In the days of the Incas in Peru, honey was offered up as a sacrifice to the sun. Babylonians erected their temples on ground that had been consecrated with honey. In India, Vishnu—one of the great triad, Brahma, Vishnu, and Siva—was represented as a blue bee resting on a lotus bloom. And Kama, the Indian god of love, was said to carry a bow the string of which was formed by a chain of bees. A belief among pagan tribes in Germany was that the bees came to earth from an underground paradise where they dwelt with the Fates.

One of the myths of ancient Greece relates how sacred bees nourished and protected the infant Zeus when he was hidden in a cave in Crete. Honey was said to have been the sole food of this future chief of the Olympian gods during infancy. In consequence, he was sometimes called The Bee Man. One day when he was lying in his cradle, according to the old myth, four men, dressed in armour, entered the cave intending to steal the honey of the sacred bees. In the presence of Zeus's cradle, their armour split at every joint and the guardian bees fell upon their unprotected bodies and drove them from the cave.

In that mine of curious facts about man's relationship to the honeybees, Hilda M. Ransome's *The Sacred Bee*, there is related a legend of Brittany which has been handed down from generation to generation. It tells how the bees were created from the tears which Christ shed on the cross. Instead of falling to the ground, each teardrop turned into a winged insect which flew away into the sunshine to bring sweetness to all mankind.

Throughout his life, Napoleon Bonaparte was fascinated by the order and efficiency of the bee state. He selected these industrious insects for use on his coat of arms and, when he was crowned Emperor, he wore a green coronation robe decorated with golden bees. More than 1,000 years before, when another European monarch, the Frankish king, Childric I, died, 300 golden bees were placed in the tomb in which he was buried.

The lore of the beekeeper, developed through centuries of apiculture, provides a fertile source of strange beliefs and superstitions. How to make bees thrive, how to avoid stings, how to control swarms—common problems such as these have produced a host of amazing receipts and rules.

In the days of the Roman Pliny the Elder a sure preventive for bee stings was the ancient counterpart of the modern rabbit's foot. "As many as have about them the bill of a woodspeck (woodpecker), when they come to take honey out of the hive," wrote this early naturalist, "shall not be stung by the bees."

Several centuries before, Greek beekeepers followed the practice of shaving their heads before working with their insects. Probably with some reason, these ancient apiculturists believed that the perfume of their hair irritated the bees and made them sting. A fact that was early known, and has since been verified by scientific study, is that honeybees are sometimes aroused by human breath. Modern manuals of beekeeping point out the wisdom of not breathing directly on the insects while the frames are being handled at a hive. In Western Pennsylvania, many years ago, there used to be a simple but difficult suggestion for avoiding bee stings which was always handed on to beginners in apiculture. It was: Hold your breath while working with the bees!

In this same part of the United States, a current belief held that redheaded people irritate bees and make them sting. Another folk belief that has been current for centuries in many parts of Europe is that immorality on the part of the beekeeper will result in arousing the bees to stinging fury. In some locations it was the custom of girls to test their suitors by leading them past a hive of bees.

Among the people of France, this idea that the honeybee is a guardian of morals as well as a producer of honey is carried still further. According to the belief of many peasants, bees sting those given to profanity as a reminder of their sins. Another idea of the French peasant is that when a man is stung it is a message from a relative in Purgatory, reminding him of his duty to offer up prayers for his relative's soul.

"Telling the bees" is an age-old custom that has spread throughout Europe and into countries where Europeans have colonized. Whittier's poem of that title, written in 1858, records the curious ritual as it was carried out in New England. Basically, the practice goes back to the idea of the close relationship between the bees and their owner. If the owner died, the insects must be told of his death or they would become offended and go away.

In Germany, France, England, and other countries, a member of the bereaved family would knock on the hive and repeat the words: "The Master is dead. The Master is dead." This would prevent the bees from flying away. In the north of France, the person informing the bees was always careful to tap the hive thrice and on the Isle of Guernsey the tapping was always done with the key of the house. If the bees answered with a hum, it was understood that they were consenting to stay and make honey for the new owner.

Black crape, or a small black piece of wood, sometimes was placed on the hive during the period of mourning. In parts of France, the hives wore these markings for six months after the death of the owner and, according to the belief of the peasants, the bees refrained from humming throughout the period.

Not only deaths, but other events in the lives of the beekeepers were often shared with the insects. They were invited to wedding feasts as well as to funerals. Their hives were decked out in red cloth when the Breton peasant, in France, was celebrating a wedding feast. In England, a still further example of the closeness of the relationship between bee owner and his bees is found in the ancient custom of informing the hive dwellers of any great public event, such as the declaration of war or the birth of a royal heir. Bees, the people of Bishopsborne used to maintain, would never thrive if important news was withheld from them.

In time of war, people of the same region believed, bees languish and do not thrive. The fact that under unsettled conditions the insects probably received less careful attention may have provided the basis for this idea. The same explanation may account for the widely held superstition that after the death of the master bees fail to prosper.

In Greece, at the time of Pericles, there were said to be 20,000 colonies of bees. For forty centuries man has been keeping these honey-producing insects. As a result, a goodly share of odd beliefs in the lore of apiculture concern the welfare of the hive.

An almost universal belief has been that stolen swarms never thrive. However, French peasants in the Vosges maintain that when too high a price is paid for bees the colony will not prosper. In Londonderry, Ireland, beekeepers have a saying that the insects must always be sold, never given away, if the receiver is to have any luck in his honey crop. However, in other parts of the British Isles it was considered unlucky to sell bees. They must always be traded for something of equal value. Another related superstition of the British Isles from comes Northumberland. To be the sole owner of bees is considered unlucky. The colonies must be owned in partnership if good fortune is to be attained. And according to the belief of people in Northampton, bees never are successful when possessed by a quarrelsome family.

In that fascinating compilation of entomological oddities Frank

Cowan's *Curious Facts in the History of Insects* there is related a superstition of early beekeepers in Pennsylvania, to the effect that no man could ever own a hundred prosperous beehives. He would have good luck with eighty or ninety or even ninety-nine colonies. But the moment the number of his hives reached the hundred mark, bad fortune would befall them.

To keep ill luck away from the bees, an infinite variety of charms and incantations have been used at various times in human history. In countries of the Near East, it once was thought that burying "the liver of a white falcon" or the eye of a bear beneath the hive was an infallible method of insuring the success of the bees within. The skull of a horse or cow is sometimes still placed on the top of a hive in the Caucasus, a relic of an ancient belief in the efficacy of such means of averting the "evil eye" from the insects.

In villages of Transylvania, a house key used to be placed before the doorway of the hive, the belief being that flying over the key makes the bees more industrious and prevents robber insects from gaining an entrance to the hive. Bedfordshire beekeepers, in England, used to stand before hives that were not doing well and sing psalms, while in central Europe pieces of volcanic rock, known as toadstone, were put beneath the hives to make the insects prosper. Stranger still was a custom of central European peasants who used to give their bees written contracts guaranteeing that they would be cherished and taken care of throughout the year!

Ever since the earliest beekeepers tried to domesticate the golden throng, a problem of apiculture has been the controlling and recovering of swarms. Strange receipts for attaining this end have ranged from beating pans to repeating charm verses in Latin. As old as Virgil and Pliny is the belief that swarming bees can be made to alight by the beating of pans and the ringing of bells. Later, this practice was continued as an announcement to neighbours that the beekeeper's hive had given off a swarm. According to the laws of the Hebrews, as recorded in *The Talmud*, when a swarm settled on a tree in a neighbour's field, the owner of the bees could cut off the limb and would have to pay only for that one bough.

When beekeepers in certain sections of England thought their insects were about to swarm, they made it a practice to stand before the hives and sing songs to amuse the bees and keep them from leaving the premises.

Many years ago, in the eastern part of the United States, a pioneer apiculturist, the Reverend Thomas P. Hunt, announced a sure aid to making swarming bees alight before they left the owner's land. It was call a "bee-bob." Using a fine needle and thread, the practitioner of the art strung dead bees together until he had enough to make a ball the size of an egg. Loose ends of thread, holding bees, were supposed to extend out from the ball. This bee-bob was then attached to the top of a long pole. When a swarm had left the hive, the pole was carried about the beeyard. The bees, seeing the ball of insects, were supposed to have their minds turned—through the power of suggestion—to clustering. Invariably, according to the deviser of the scheme, they would go and do likewise!

Getting the swarm to enter a new hive and insuring the bees would remain there formed the bases of two curious bits of activity in England. Peasants in Gloucester used to turn an empty hive upside down, pour a quart of beans in it, and then let a sow eat the beans. Immediately afterwards, they believed, the swarm would settle on the hive and make it their home. In Cornwall it used to be the custom to rub the inside of a hive into which a new swarm was being placed with so-called "scrawnsey buds" or elder flowers. This procedure was supposed to keep the insects from deserting their new dwelling place.

Frequently in the past, the issuance of a swarm—so mysterious and exciting in character—has been viewed by the superstitious as an omen. In Ireland, the swarming of bees was once believed to prognosticate a death in the family of the owner. If the bees alighted on rotten wood, this fact was considered by peasants of East Norfolk, in England, to indicate the same misfortune. The Greeks thought that the issuance of a swarm indicated a stranger was coming, and in Switzerland, according to an old history, the approach of an attacking "forain army" was rightly foretold by the common people when they saw a swarm of bees that "flew to the town and there sate upon the tyles" of a rooftop.

Among the Romans, it was often thought that swarms foretold misfortune. Sixty-four years after the birth of Christ, the populace in Rome was upset by forebodings of evil when a swarm settled on the capitol. Scipio refused to advance in war after a swarm had alighted on his tent, and it was believed that the death of the Emperor Claudius was foretold by a swarm that settled in his camp.

The exact spot where a swarm alights has been considered of great importance in detecting the approach of future events. Thus, in Switzerland, if the bees choose a dry limb or twig as their resting place, it means that a sick person in the house of the owner will die. If a swarm settled on a house in Austria, the fact used to be viewed as a lucky omen. And once, when the throne of Poland was vacant, a candidate was chosen as king on the basis of the fact that a swarm of bees alighted on him while the election was being held. The superstitious considered it an omen that he would be a lucky monarch.

It is obvious that the sooner a swarm establishes its new home and begins making honey the greater will be the year's harvest for the beekeeper. A folk-lore jingle which has been repeated for generations expressed the ideas: "A swarm in May is worth a load of hay. A swarm in June is worth a silver spoon. A swarm in July is not worth a fly." Swarms on Good Friday had special significance. In one section of Germany, peasants believed that a farmer who drove his cattle to market with a bough on which bees had settled in a swarm on Good Friday, and which later was cut to form a cross, would find a ready sale for his livestock.

In the less civilized corners of the world, bees, as well as their honey, have been used as an article of diet. According to the author of an old travel book, natives in the Caribbean Islands were in the habit of eating young bees " rawe, roasted, and sometimes sodden." An explorer friend of mind once sampled a dish which African tribesmen greatly relish. It is formed of raw honeybee grubs. In Ceylon, a flaming torch would be held under a cluster of swarming bees, singeing their wings and causing them to drop to the ground. Here they were eagerly gathered up by the natives. Carried home, they were boiled and eaten. Bees, roasted in oil, and smeared on the hair, provided an ancient Assyrian receipt for keeping hair from turning white.

Magic medicinal virtues have often been attributed to the honey produced by bees. In India, an ancient rite is performed after the birth of a male child. The father recites these words as he offers a small amount of honey: "I give thee this honey food so that the gods may protect thee and that thou mayest live a hundred autumns in this world." In other parts of the globe—in Greece, Germany, Palestine—children were also fed bits of honey immediately after birth.

In the Far East, bees were called the " Birds of the Muses." The idea that they have the power to impart eloquence to a child of their choice has prevailed through centuries in many parts of the world. Plato, Sophocles, and Xenophon, all have been known as "The Athenian Bee" or "The Bee of Attica" because of the sweetness of their style and the belief that bees alighted or swarmed on their mouths when they were infants. St. Ambrose, according to the legend, was visited by bees when he was lying in a cradle in his father's courtyard. Afterward, the bees rose so high in the air they vanished from sight. This, according to *The Lives of the Saints*, was taken to presage his future greatness and eloquence. Creoles, in former days, are said to have believed they could see into the future if their bodies were coated with honey, and heathen tribes in early Lithuania predicted future events from the shapes formed when melted beeswax was poured into cold water.

In the sixth century B.C., the Greek philosopher, Pythagoras, preached the life-giving properties of honey. His followers believed that if they ate honey for breakfast each day they would be free from diseases throughout their lives. Pythagoras himself lived to a great age, attributing his longevity to his regular habit of eating honey.

Even after death, the Greeks sometimes used honey to preserve the body of the deceased. It is said that Democritus, the philosopher, was buried in honey and that the body of Alexander the Great was similarly interred. The marvellous preservative effect of this fluid is indicated by the fact that preparations for the state funerals of potentates in India sometimes required a full year, during which time the body was kept encased in honey. Kings in Scythia, according to the Greek historian Herodotus, were buried with their bodies enclosed not in honey but in beeswax.

Arabs believed that honey had especial value for treating the eyes. They also thought that it should be given to a dog, immediately after it had been bitten by another dog, to insure speedy healing of the wounds. Mead, the honey drink of ancient Europe, a beverage that antedated beer, was believed to bring the gifts of song and prophecy, and to be the drink of the dead warrior heroes in Valhalla. It was produced by the fermentation of a mixture of honey and water. Later, spices or wine were sometimes added to the golden-yellow beverage. In some parts of Europe, cowslip honey was considered best for making mead.

The vast quantities of this honey liquor consumed in the Middle Ages can be gauged from one instance recorded in *The Sacred Bee*. In 1015, a fire broke out in Meissen, on the Upper Elbe, during a shortage of water. The inhabitants extinguished the blaze by pouring over the flames large quantities of mead! The term "honeymoon" is reported to date from the days of the mead drinkers. An old Teuton custom was to drink mead for thirty days after a wedding.

The origin of the honeybees, as has been pointed out, was a riddle for many centuries. The most widely accepted theory was that they were generated within the decaying carcasses of noble animals. Samson's famous riddle, as given in the Book of Judges, in the Bible, reflects this belief: "Out of the eater came forth meat, out of the strong came forth sweetness." The answer: "What is sweeter than honey, what is stronger than a lion," revealed the common belief that bees originated in the body of a dead lion.

Oxen, rather than lions, were usually considered as the producers of bees. Virgil in the fourth *Georgic* explains how to kill an ox, how to sprinkle the floor on which the carcass is placed with herbs, and finally how to watch for the swarm of bees that will appear. According to another Roman writer of an early day, the ox-born worker bees were created from the flesh of the animal while the "king" bees came from the brain or spinal marrow. The simple explanation of this widely held misconception as to the birth of the bees is that flies, which closely resemble bees at first glance, swarm about such a carcass and lay their eggs on the decaying flesh.

Another curious belief that was handed down from writer to

writer in antiquity has just as simple an explanation. In rough boisterous weather, bees were thought to pick up tiny stones and carry them as ballast. Plutarch, writing a century before the birth of Christ, reported: "The bees of Candi, being about to double a point or cape lying into the sea, which is much exposed to the winds, they ballast themselves with small grit or petty stones, for to be able to endure the weather and not be carried away against their wills with the winds through their lightness otherwise." About a century later, Virgil expressed the same notion in his *Georgics*:

> And as when empty barks on billows float,
> With sandy ballast sailors trim the boat,
> So bees bear gravel stones whose poising weight,
> Steers through the whistling winds their steady flight.

It was the Dutch naturalist, Jan Swammerdam, who first pointed out the mistake of the ancient writers. In place of honeybees, they had seen wild mason bees bringing home their little loads of mud and gravel with which they created their nests.

In all the lore of beekeeping, probably the most picturesque character was the Englishman, Daniel Wildman. Known as Wildman, The Bee Man, he travelled about through Europe, exhibiting his mastery over his insect swarms at about the time of the American Revolution. It was recorded that at his command his bees would settle on his head, his beard, or any other part of his body he designated. The Barnum of the Beekeepers, his colourful exhibitions made him famous and brought requests to demonstrate his ability at several of the courts of Europe. Once he was carried through London in a chair almost completely covered with bees. Wildman is said to have tamed wasps and hornets as well as bees. His most spectacular feat was his reported battle against three mastiffs when he was armed only with swarms of honey-

NECTAR HUNTERS among apple blossoms. By placing insect-proof cages around two adjacent trees and liberating bees in one, a New Jersey scientist discovered that the pollen-carrying work of the bees increased the fruit yield forty-fold.

THE OLD-FASHIONED STRAW SKEP was used for centuries to house bees and is still employed in some parts of the world. In Britain and the U.S.A., it has almost entirely disappeared, the movable-frame hive having taken its place.

HIVING A SWARM is accomplished in many ways, the method used depending upon the circumstances. In this instance, the cluster had been placed

in a paper carton the evening before when it was too late to transfer it to a permanent home. The bees remained in this temporary shelter overnight. This series of pictures shows the steps used in trans-

ferring the thousands of insects to their new home. Close beside the carton, the beekeeper places the foundation for the hive. On it he sets the main sec-

tion of the hive, equipped with movable frames. When all is in readiness, he lifts the carton above the empty frames and shakes out a cascade of living insects. With the queen, the bees quickly make their way downward through the open top of the hive and begin the work of establishing a new insect city. From then on, the swarm accepts the hive as its

home and makes no move to leave it. Soon the bees are engaging in the familiar activities of brood rearing and nectar gathering, guarding the entrance and

ventilating the interior. Sometimes the bees are simply dumped in front of the entrance of a new hive and permitted to find their way inside. In either

case, the beekeeper, as shown here, leaves his insects permanently settled in a new home, thus bringing to an end the excitement of swarming time.

MODERN hives, equipped with movable frames, provide present-day bees with better working conditions for the production of honey. Such frames were first devised by the pioneer American apiculturist, Lorenzo L. Langstroth.

HE HAS A GRANDFATHER BUT NO FATHER. Drones hatch from unfertilized eggs, hence have only one parent, the queen. But she came from a fertilized egg and had both father and mother. Thus the fatherless drone has a grandfather.

HOLIDAY MOOD. Bees, ordinarily quick to resent familiarity, will often permit themselves to be handled or ladled about with a spoon when in a swarm. Swarming time is the one holiday, the one play-day, they know.

INSECT FURNACE. By forming a cluster and producing heat by muscular exertion, bees are able to maintain a winter temperature that sometimes reaches a point 75 degrees F. above that of the outer atmosphere. The cluster expands or contracts according to whether the thermometer goes up or down.

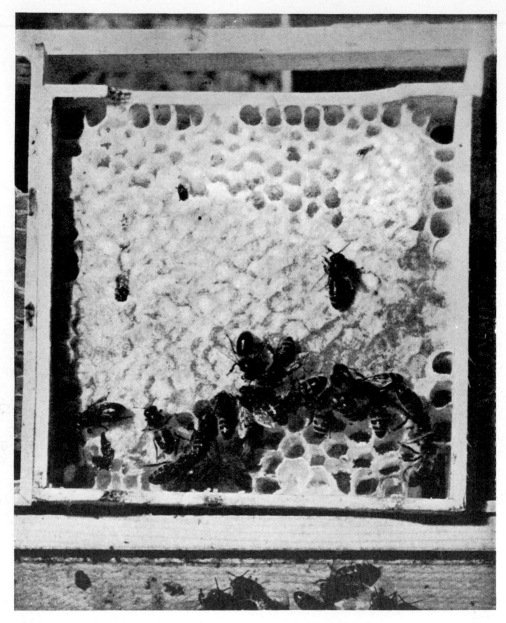

SUMMER SAVINGS, in the form of concentrated honey, provides the bank balance of the thrifty bees, sustaining them through the long, cold weeks of winter.

AUTUMN ASTERS provide most of the nectar carried to the hive just before frost. Bees, visiting flowers, travel about 15 miles an hour. When they are carrying loads of nectar to the hive, they maintain about the same speed.

LAST SWEETS OF AUTUMN are often the juices of fallen fruit. Because the smooth jaws of workers are unsuited for cutting fruit skins, the insects are never guilty of damaging orchard products. Only when fruit is damaged, as above, do bees suck out the juices as a final source of autumn honey.

PATTERNS form and dissolve as two negatives of the same honeycomb are moved about, one in front of the other. On the next two pages, half a dozen of

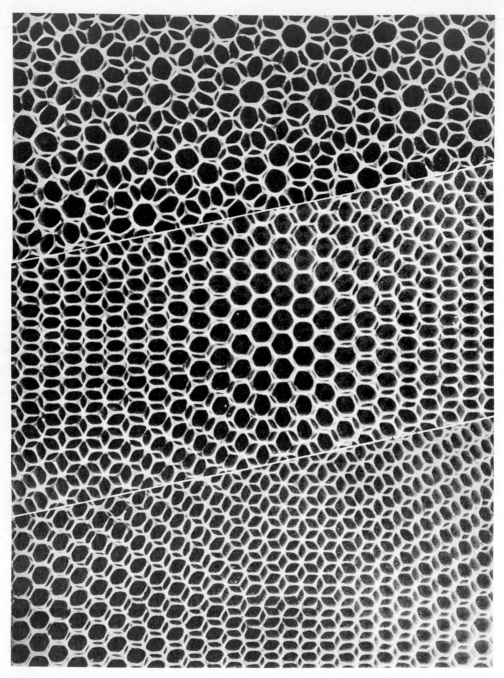

these honeycomb-pattern pictures are shown. They are recorded by placing
the two films in the enlarger at the same time. So exact is the average honeycomb

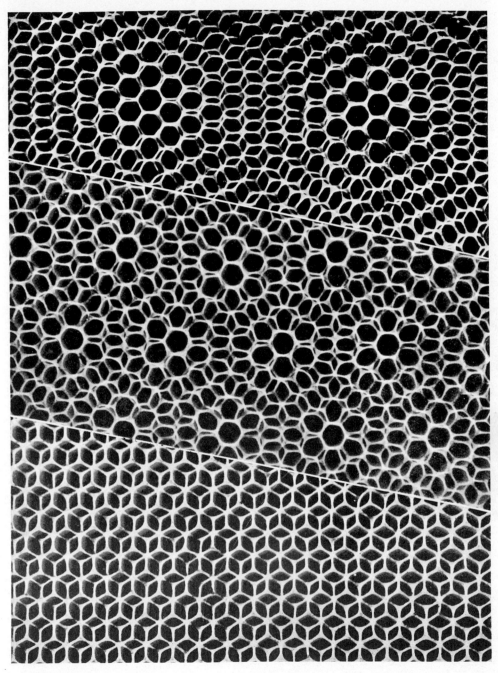

cell that the famous French scientist, Réaumur, early in the Eighteenth Century proposed that it be adopted in Europe as a standard unit of measure.

WINTER OVERCOATS for beehives, in the form of a wrapping of black tar paper, are provided to help conserve the energy of the insects during winter months.

bees. According to old writers, he sent forth his bees as each dog rushed toward him. Thus he vanquished them all, the bees stinging the animals until they fled from the scene of the singular encounter.

Bees instead of bullets have been employed in many wars, from the siege of Henry I by the Duke of Lorraine—when beehives, hurled among the horses of the followers of the Duke, resulted in their rout—to the World War of 1914-18—when German troops in East Africa used bees to fight the British. In Labour disputes in America, bees have also been used for the discomfiture of guards and pickets.

Honey mines in Texas and honey birds in Africa provide two additional oddity-items that belong in any compilation of queer facts connected with bees. David Livingstone mentioned the bird, *Cuculus indicator*, nearly a century ago and many scientists have studied it since on African explorations. It is said to lead people by its cries to the tree where bees have their stores of honey. Dr James Chapin, in an article in *Natural History Magazine,* some time ago, reported that these pilot birds are in the habit of leading honey badgers to bee trees. After the animals tear open the wood and dine on the honey within, the birds obtain some of the sweets that are left. This strange relationship between bird and animal has been extended to include man. It explains the amazing instances in which humans have been led through the African jungles to bee trees.

This authenticated bird story has a basis of truth. Yet it is just as fantastic as the imaginary tale of vast honey mines in the caves of Texas. This legend keeps cropping up from time to time under different conditions. In essence it is always the same. Some prospector has entered a lonely cave and has found that it has been used for centuries by the bees for storing honey. There are thousands of tons of this liquid gold there for the taking. In one instance, at least, stock in such an imaginary mine was offered to gullible honey lovers as a get-rich quick road to wealth.

Two other tall tales, one from China and the other from the Middle West, will complete this record of honeybee lore. Among the K'un-lun Mountains, so the Oriental tale goes, there resides a giant race of bees. Each insect is ten feet long and its sting is so powerful that when it is thrust through the hide of an elephant the great brute drops dead as though struck by lightning! The story from the Middle West, a typical bit of American humour, relates how a politically minded apiarist crossed an American eagle with a bumble-bee. The result was a pure strain of Presidential Bee.

14

BOOKS AND BEES

IN the next to the last year of the nineteenth century, the Belgian dramatist Maurice Maeterlinck left Paris to spend the summer in a secluded country house, set among the grainfields and orchards of Normandy. The winter before, his mystical essays, *Wisdom and Destiny*, had first appeared in print. The idea of writing a life of the bee was remote from Maeterlinck's mind.

One morning, sitting beneath beech trees beside the square, whitewashed dwelling, he read again some pages from one of the wild-bee books of Jean Henri Fabre. "What marvels could be written about all that!" he exclaimed as he laid down the volume. A few days later, so Georgette Leblanc tells us, Maeterlinck sat down at a heavy wooden table covered with a green cloth and there began those first beguilingly simple pages of his entomological classic, *La Vie des Abeilles* (*The Life of the Bee*).

The book literally was written among the insects it celebrates. Through the open windows, bees came on blurring wings, attracted by the coloured saucers of honey which Maeterlinck placed on the green cloth cover of his table. In its bibliography, his volume lists the main authorities of his day. Yet there is no smell of the library in *The Life of the Bee*. Rather the scent of the open fields and the redolence of honey and wax pervade its pages. It is, in fact, "an account of the bees' short year from April to the last days of September, told by one who loves them and knows them." But it is more. Always, Maeterlinck keeps coming back to man and the mysteries of his existence. The enigmas in the life of the bee and in the life of man go hand in hand throughout the pages of his book. No other volume in all entomological literature has received equal acclaim or has been so widely read.

In more recent years, the ingenious researches of von Frisch and other scientists have given us new insight into the events of the hive. Such information was, of course, unknown to Maeterlinck. But to-day, nearly half a century after *The Life of the Bee* was written, the main facts are accurate as Maeterlinck set them down. His volume combines essential accuracy with beauty of expression and a full feeling for the drama and poetry which surround the life of these social insects. Like a juncture of rivers, where the waters mingle and form one stream, his book brings science and literature together. *The Life of the Bee* is one of those rare volumes which can be read for its beauty, its fact, or both.

It was years ago, in a dune-county garden where great pink and white mallows formed colourful banquet halls for honeybees, that I first began to read this remarkable book. From the matter-of-fact, almost statistical beginning, page by page, there unfolded the full drama of these insects whose endless murmur filled the air around me. I still have in my library that same treasured volume, its green cover rain-stained by a sudden summer shower of long ago.

This bee classic of the Belgian dramatist and mystic belongs at the top of the list of volumes for the bee lover's library. It is a book to own, to read, and to read again. But, in addition, there are many other volumes to choose from. If I were but to list all the works which have been written about bees, it would require a book far larger than the present volume. In 1646, when the ancient writer, De Montford, produced *The Portrait of the Honey-Fly*, he estimated that between 500 and 600 authors before him had written volumes about bees. Several years ago, E. F. Phillips, then of the U.S. Department of Agriculture, reported that the total number of bee books in existence exceeded 20,000. Of all the insects, the honeybee has been the most studied, the most written about.

Aristotle, the early Greek philosopher, was one of the first to leave a treatise on the subject. Pliny the Elder, in the days of the Emperor Vesputian, compiled an illuminating record of what was known or imagined about this honey-making insect. Virgil celebrated the bee in his *Georgics*.

Of all these early writers, Pliny was the most unusual. He was, in fact, one of the most remarkable men of his time. After working a good part of the night, he would arise at dawn to attend the Emperor. After a light breakfast, he would lie in the sun while a secretary read to him. His sun bath was followed by a cold plunge. Then he lunched and took a short nap. As soon as he awoke, he resumed his studies. During the dinner hour, a secretary read while Pliny ate. Every book, he used to say, no matter how bad, contained some fragment of merit, something worth remembering. Even when he went abroad, Pliny had a secretary by his side reading aloud. Thus, by using every waking moment to best advantage, by budgeting his time, by maintaining a rigorous schedule of work and self-discipline, he was able to produce more than one hundred volumes, including his record of the honeybee, during the fifty-six years of his life. In 79 A.D. the eruption of Vesuvius, which wiped out Pompeii, brought death to Pliny.

Centuries after these pioneer writers there appeared that quartette of great European bee men: Swammerdam, Réaumur, Huber, and Lubbock.

Jan Swammerdam, a Dutch naturalist of the eighteenth century, with plodding thoroughness, solved many of the problems which had puzzled previous observers. The records of his researches were, for the most part, confined to scientific publications. However, his contributions to our understanding of life in the hive are outstanding and his name should be included in any list of writers on the subject of the honeybee.

In France, that versatile scientist René Antoine Ferchault de Réaumur was known as "The Historian of the Bees." Réaumur—inventor of a thermometer, pioneer in the artificial incubation of eggs, discoverer of new methods in the production of steel and the manufacture of tinware—was a painstaking student of the insects. As late as 1928, Dr William Morton Wheeler, of Harvard University, translated a manuscript on ants which Réaumur left unpublished at his death. Appearing 171 years later, it proved that this French scientist had antedated later researches in many of his experiments with these insects. His *Natural History of the Bees* is one of the great classics in its field.

It was the Swiss naturalist François Huber, however, whose discoveries revealed to the world the full wonder and drama of the hive. He showed that in the bee's city of wax reality is as surprising as anything imagined by the earliest writers. Blind from the age of fifteen years, Huber made up for his seemingly insurmountable handicap by the ingenuity and resourcefulness of his mind and the thoroughness of his methods. He was aided in his work by an ever-faithful servant, François Burnens, and by his wife, Marie Lullin.

The record of Huber's investigations—researches which laid the foundation for our scientific knowledge of the intimate life of the hive—was published in Geneva, Switzerland, in 1792. Fourteen years later it was translated into English. This classic volume was written in the form of a series of letters and is called *New Observations on the Natural History of Bees*. Born in 1750, Huber died in 1831. Physically blind, he saw more clearly into the existence of the bees than any man before him.

A few years ago, in a cubicle cubbyhole at the back of a second-hand book-store on lower Fourth Avenue, in New York City, I came upon a thin volume with stained pages and a leather backing more than a century old. When I opened the book, the first sentence that struck my eye read: "If a ftranger queen appears, fhe is inftantly feized by the bees on guard." Throughout the book, many "s's" were printed like "f's" in the old-fashioned way. The title page contained the following: "New Observations on the Natural History of Bees, by François Huber. Translated from the original. Edinburgh, 1806." I had stumbled on one of the original volumes which came from those old-time presses that had printed the earliest English translation of Huber's masterpiece. For a single dollar, I purchased the prize and carried it home.

Sir John Lubbock, the British bee observer, like Pliny, was a man of affairs. His classic experiments with bees and ants and wasps—experiments which stimulated others to follow in his footsteps—were performed at odd moments during a life of action in England. The record of his researches is contained in his volume, *Ants, Bees and Wasps.*

Eleven years before Lubbock was born, another great historian of the insects, Jean Henri Fabre, began life in a peasant's cottage in the south of France. Throughout the ninety-two years of Fabre's existence, poverty was always close behind. For twenty years, at a salary that never exceeded £80 a year, he worked as schoolteacher in Avignon. All during these two seemingly barren decades he was carrying on his historic researches into the ways of the insects, using the crudest of home-made apparatus.

After more than forty years of penury, Fabre accumulated savings sufficient to purchase a tiny foothold of land, a pebble-strewn, thistly "harmas" at Serignan, in Provence. Here he continued his painstaking researches, recording in his simple, charming style the wonders he observed. Charles Darwin called Fabre "the incomparable observer." Victor Hugo termed him "the Homer of the

Insects." And Maurice Maeterlinck declared Fabre was "the most profound admiration" of his life. On his ninetieth birthday, representatives of the French government and various learned societies assembled at Serignan to honour Fabre. With characteristic simplicity, he looked over the assembled dignitaries and remarked dryly to a friend: "I must be very strange to look at for so many people to come such distances to see me!"

The long series of books that came from Fabre's pen are known collectively as *Souvenirs Entomologiques*. The two that most concern those interested in the hive are *The Mason Bees* and *Bramble-Bees and Others*. Both of these volumes help us to understand the wild relatives of the honeybee. In the fall of 1915, Fabre's long life came to an end. His span of years bridges the gap between the entomological writers of yesterday and those of to-day.

Among the hundreds of modern books in the field of apiculture, it is possible to mention but a few. For those who wish a condensed and simple exposition of the bee's way of life, several volumes may be consulted: *The Outline of Science*, edited by J. Arthur Thomson; *Handbook of Nature Study*, by Anna Botsford Comstock; and *Our Insect Friends and Foes and Spiders*, published by the National Geographic Society. Younger readers will find an introduction to the wonders of the hive in such volumes as *The Bee People*, by Margaret W. Morley, and *Cities of Wax*, by Julie C. Kenly.

Two volumes that contain a vast amount of interesting information about bees and their long relationship with man are: *The Sacred Bee*, by Hilda M. Ransome, and *Honey and Health*, by Bodog F. Beck. A third volume, unfortunately long out of print, is Frank Cowan's *Curious Facts in the History of Insects*. While this author was stationed in Washington, D. C., during the Civil War, he beguiled tedious hours by poring over old and odd books at the Congressional Library, compiling a compendium of curious facts about insects. One of the best chapters in the book is on the lore of the honeybee.

Dr Beck's book, referred to a moment ago, in addition to its lore about bees, gives the most complete available information about the health-giving properties of honey and the therapeutic use of bee venom. A never-to-be-forgotten evening was one during which I watched this physician-author, a bee buzzing loudly at the end of a tongslike holding instrument, apply the sting to the swollen hand of one of his rheumatic patients.

If you are interested in learning more of the practical aspects of bee raising, two indispensable volumes are: *Beekeeping*, by E. F. Phillips, and *The ABC and XYZ of Bee Culture*, by A. I. and E. R. Root. An astonishing amount of interesting fact and practical information is packed between the covers of Phillips's medium-sized book. His years as head of the apiculture bureau of the Department of Agriculture, in Washington, D.C., provided him with the vast amount of material which he has condensed into a single volume.

The Root volume has grown with the years. The story is told that one summer day in 1871 A. I. Root, a manufacturing jeweller of Medina, Ohio, saw a swarm pass overhead. One of his work-men offered to retrieve the bees for a dollar. Out of that casual event grew Root's interest in beekeeping. The company he later formed to manufacture apicultural supplies has become a unique institution which has had much to do with the spread of interest in bee raising in the United States. The *ABC and XYZ* is an ency-clopedia of information arranged in alphabetical order. Since it was first published in 1877, more than 200,000 copies have been printed. Again and again, it has been re-issued, expanded, and revised. It represents a seemingly endless source of information about the insects and their care.

For readers who are interested in going beyond the hive and

becoming acquainted with the strange wild relatives of the honey-bees, there are several books of identification and factual information that will be of assistance, notably Frank E. Lutz's *Fieldbook of Insects* and Leland O. Howard's *The Insect Book*. The *Fieldbook* has the advantage of compactness, being just the right size to slip into a coat pocket for ready reference. Its pages have provided light for thousands of amateur explorers in the realm of the insects.

The life of the familiar bumblebee is made clearer by Otto Emil Plath's *Bumblebees and Their Ways*. Besides describing the different American species, the book contains many observations on their activity and habits. The author kept scores of colonies of these insects in small cigar-box observation hives on the ledges of his windows, where he could watch their actions day or night. In two of William Morton Wheeler's volumes, *The Social Insects* and *Social Life among the Insects*, the reader will find helpful information about bees and their place in the insect world.

The botanical aspects of apiculture are taken up in a number of volumes, such as John H. Lovell's *Honey Plants of North America* and Frank C. Pellett's *American Honey Plants*. The intricate internal structure of the bee is revealed by R. E. Snodgrass's monumental *The Anatomy and Physiology of the Honeybee*. This classic volume was the product of years of delicate, microscopic dissection.

The most recent investigations into the ways of the bees, such as those of von Frisch, have been reported in various scientific publications. H. G. Wells's *The Science of Life* gives a summary of von Frisch's discoveries, while the *Annual Report of the Smithsonian Institution* for 1938 includes a paper by this scientist on the results of his work. A slender volume, *Social Behaviour in Insects*, by A. D. Imms, provides a clear, condensed résumé of science's present-day understanding of the forces that govern life in the hive.

Among the red, brown, blue, and green volumes standing upright on shelves near my observation hive are most of the books mentioned in this chapter. I am including at the end of this volume a bibliography covering additional titles which, for lack of space, I have been unable to include here.

Beyond that extended list, however, there stretches the vast forest of books which have been printed in the past on the subject of bees and their social life. Exploring these printed pages is an occupation for winter months—for that long succession of weeks when cold has come; when honey making and brood rearing, swarming and comb building, have come to a standstill and the feverish activity of summer is over.

15

WINTER

FOR several days now, my bees have come tacking home in boisterous autumn winds. Ironweed and goldenrod and waving purple asters fill the upland fields. At night, migrating birds cross the disc of the full moon, and under a midday sky, hard like blue steel, dragonflies dart upward from among the weeds with a dry rattle of parchment wings. Heavy dews and morning fogs and the far-carrying scent of burning leaves tell of autumn's coming.

To-day, yellows and golds, russets and browns, stretch across the valley. In only a few weeks, heavy skies and clouds rolling low from the west with cold driving rains will strip the branches. The days of abundance are ending. On the stage of the insect world, beyond my hive, the drama is over and the brown curtain of autumn is descending.

Already the populous nests of the wasp, the hornet, and the bumblebee are deserted. The legion singers of the night, the crickets, the grasshoppers, the katydids, soon will be stilled by early frosts. Only the prudent ant and the provident bee, among the unnumbered millions of summer insects, will continue their communal life through the dark and cheerless weeks of winter.

In this conclusion to the story of the bees, there are the overtones of a fairy-tale ending. The frugal reap the reward of their industry ; the improvident die in want. The surplus, saved from summer days, maintains life through the bleakness of winter. The greedy, indolent drones come to a bad end while the industrious workers live on, snug and warm in the waxen city which their labours have created.

In that strange rebellion of the workers, the so-called massacre of the drones, a primal law of Nature is functioning. The useful prevail; the useless perish. In days of easy plenty, when nectar in abundance is flowing into the hive, the golden throng supports the sluggards of the colony without complaint. But when the honey flow is over or when shortening days and fading flowers tell that autumn has come, their attitude suddenly alters. The burden of these unproductive, oversize members of the colony—now their sole excuse for living is gone—would jeopardize the safety of the hive. Without hesitation, the workers turn against the pampered drones. The law of Nature is carried out; the useless perish.

From the viewpoint of the drones, this sudden shift in attitude must be an incomprehensible, bewildering piece of treachery. The friends they have taken for granted, overnight, become enemies bent on their destruction. Occurring most often in late summer and early autumn, this change may take place as early as July. It is always presaged by the same event, the drying up of the nectar supply. In periods of sudden drought, when the honey flow unexpectedly slackens, the bees oftentimes turn on the drones and drive them from the hive.

For autumn bees, the tiniest flower is none too small; they journey farther and farther afield to fill their honey bags. As the main supply of nectar begins to fail, however, the drops of honey fed the drones seem to be given with greater and greater reluctance. The bees figuratively count their pennies, reckon profit and loss, begrudge the wasteful drones their appetites.

In fact, the behaviour of the bees toward the drones has been called a barometer of conditions among the flowers in the fields. Several cases have been reported in which colonies rid themselves of the drones during the lull between the blooming of apple orchards and the honey flow in white-clover fields. At the other extreme, drones are sometimes permitted to remain in the hive until late in the autumn, and, in the instance of queenless colonies, they have been retained through the winter. But such cases are the exception to the rule and occur only under abnormal conditions. In preparation for their life-and-death gamble with winter cold, one of the first acts of the bees is to rid themselves of the useless males.

At one time, it was believed that these unwelcome brothers were stung to death by the workers. Sometimes you see a drone making a desperate effort to escape while a worker buzzes along on its back, apparently attempting to drive home its sting. It is now thought that this is largely a game of bluff. A blockade, rather than a direct onslaught, is the usual technique of the workers. They range themselves to form a living barricade and hamper the movements of the drone. They cut off the food supply. And sometimes they grasp the burly males by the legs and drag them beyond the threshold of the hive.

Thus, menaced by the very bees that only the day before had fed them from the stores of the colony, the disconsolate drones take flight, only to return again to the one source of food they know. The drone, through ages of disuse, has lost the ability as well as the instinct to obtain nectar from flowers. The curled, sucking tongue of the worker bee, so important in the economy of the hive, is not possessed by the males.

Without nourishment they rapidly lose their strength. Each time they near the hive, guards rush at them menacingly or bar the way to the honey vaults within. Merciless executors of Nature's law, they prevent the drones from entering until, famished and dying, the helpless males crawl feebly among the grass-blades or in the dust before the threshold of their former home.

Drones that become too feeble to move are sometimes picked up at the entrance to the hive and carried some distance away and then dropped to the ground. The blurring wings of the worker bees, who perform this remarkable feat of lifting, are supporting a load more than twice that of the bee itself.

While the males numbly await the approaching end, predatory insects often terminate their misery by a direct attack. Another factor in hastening the end of the drones is the chill of autumn nights. Of all the members of the golden throng, the males seem most in need of warmth. They will be found, many times, clustering near the brood comb, within the hive, where the heat is greatest. So the cold of the outer atmosphere provides a quick-acting, merciful anaesthetic for these ejected bees.

In the death of the drones, the colony reaches a turning point in its economy—the transition from the accumulation of summer to the conservation of winter, from harvest to hoarding. Flowers are fast disappearing. Falling fruit, with damaged skins, attracts the bees to a new source of fluid sweets. Only when apples or grapes are split or cracked will these honey hunters attempt to suck up the juices within. The mistaken idea that bees damage fruit is disproved, as we have seen, by the simple fact that the workers have smooth jaws, unfitted and unable to tear or cut the skins. After the fruit harvest is over and the last tarnished bloom of the goldenrod has disappeared from the hillsides, the colony settles down to a routine of saving and relative inactivity. Upon the success of this struggle to conserve food and maintain warmth depends the outcome of their battle against the hazards of winter.

Rid of the luxury of the drones, they begin the final preparations for the months of cold. The queen has been laying fewer and fewer eggs. Now she often ceases her labours entirely. The nurse bees, in turn, are freed from the work of feeding the grubs. The nectar hunters compress their voyages afield into a few, midday, sunny hours. The loads they carry home grow steadily lighter. Even after frosts have killed the last of the hardy flowers, the insects still go abroad on cleansing flights. Such quick trips beyond the threshold of the hive will be continued, during thaws and brilliant sunny days when the thermometer rises, throughout the winter.

Some years ago, a scientist calculated that it requires 480 pounds of honey to maintain an average-sized colony through the twelve months of the year. Four hundred pounds of this total are required to support the bees themselves, seventy pounds to feed the brood, and ten pounds for the production of wax. This total, calculating 37,000 trips afield for each pound of stored honey, represents an almost astronomical number of journeys beyond the threshold of the hive: 17,760,000. The product of these endless comings and goings, stored away in thousands of hexagonal waxen vaults, comprises the summer savings of the bees, the bank balance upon which they are now free to draw.

Beyond the days of Indian summer—with their floating spider-silk and hazy skies—the chill brings the insects together into the golden masses in which they spend the winter. The bees, so to speak, live in the furnace room of the hive. They leave the close-packed mass of insects only to crawl to the honeycomb for nourishment or to make quick cleansing flights abroad on warmer days.

The intense, straining activity of summer is replaced by relative sloth. The busy bee, the far-ranging insect, ever on the go, spends the months of winter almost entirely within an area of no more than a square foot. The scene of its activity is bounded by the narrow corridors of the hive until spring once more unlocks the door of the open fields.

16

PHOTOGRAPHIC POSTSCRIPT

ANYONE interested in the photography of insects will find the life of the hive a fertile field for the exercise of his hobby. Bees are numerous. They are near at hand. They are infinitely varied in their activity. The spice of danger—a certain element of risk in dealing with an armed and excitable subject— adds a sporting element to the endeavour. Bees, along with the wasps and the hornets, represent the lions and tigers of the little-game jungles explored by the insect photographer.

By scientific experiment—which frequently is but another name for trying and finding out whether you get stung—I have discovered the inadvisability of wearing dark or black clothes when photographing bees.

Early one morning, I drove over to a friend's apple-orchard apiary to take a series of pictures of nurse bees at work on the brood comb. I had slipped on a black woollen shirt before starting. Within five minutes after I set up my camera, four bees had stung me and a fifth was working downward, full speed ahead, through my hair. The insects had apparently mistaken me for their hereditary enemy, the black bear!

After I made a quick, discretion-is-the-better-part-of-valour retreat to my car, washed off the stung places, and slipped into a light shirt, the insects paid little attention to me. Since then, I have noticed that the bees frequently dart viciously at my camera, evidently irritated by its black metal and leather. Experienced beekeepers have observed that black dogs or hens are much more likely to be attacked and stung by the bees in an apiary than white ones.

Besides dressing in white or light-coloured clothes, it is well to wear a hat and to slip bicycle clips or a rubber band around the bottom of your trouser legs. If a bee gets into your hair, it immediately attempts to work downward and sting. Again, if a bee crawls up your leg, it is likely to tickle and your instinctive act, in a moment of forgetfulness, may be to scratch the tickle. The result will be sudden and disastrous.

If you are stung, wash off the spot after scraping away the sting with a fingernail or knife blade. Never pull out a sting between the thumb and forefinger, as you would a thorn. In so doing, you squeeze the venom sac and force the poison into the wound. The smell of venom, if you fail to wash off the spot where you have been stung, excites the bees and may result in further stings. In addition, move as deliberately as you can and avoid jarring the insects. In taking some pictures, I have made adjustments on the lens within a few inches of thousands of the insects moving about on the comb, without any sign of animosity being shown by the bees. It might be mentioned that different colonies have different degrees of length and shortness in the matter of temper. So it is well to know your bees before you take liberties with them.

During the past three years, in recording the life of the hive on film, I have taken more than six hundred action photographs. The insects have been patient and long-suffering and my stings have been proportionately few. The best time for bee photography, I have found, is between 10:00 A.M. and 2:00 P.M. on a bright, warm day. Then the insects are in their best humour and will endure indignities they would resent at other times. Their tempers are shortest on chilly and rainy days.

One photograph that required considerable preparation, not to mention screwing up my resolution to the sticking point, shows a worker bee "committing suicide" by stinging. No one, so far as I could find out, had snapped that picture before. To complete a series, I planned a close-up of the bee pulling the sting from its body after having jabbed it into the thumb of a victim. Under the circumstances, it seemed only right that I should supply the thumb.

Drawing a line on the edge of a table, I placed an object about the size of my thumb on it and focussed the camera. Then, with photoflashes laid out and all in readiness, I held my thumb on the line—with feelings somewhat akin to those of a man putting his head on the executioner's block—and placed a pugnacious worker bee in the desired position. Without a second's delay, the bee co-operated to the limit. I set off flashes with my free hand while my wife clicked the shutter. Yet so quickly did the enraged insect move that we were able to record only two pictures before it was gone. While I placed soothing cloths on my swelling thumb, I took what consolation I could from the fact that the film-pack in my camera contained a pair of unique pictures, forming an entomological "photographic first."

The camera I used in all my work among the bees is a sturdy $3\frac{1}{4}$ by $4\frac{1}{4}$ inch film-pack outfit. A ground-glass back permits sharp focussing and a double-extension bellows enables me to get close to my tiny subjects and so record the image in sufficient size to show detail.

By adding a one-inch lens and a supplementary wide-angle lens to my equipment, I have obtained a compact outfit which records bees and other insects at from less than actual size to magnification of a dozen diameters. These four stages are represented as follows:

(1) The camera, with the double-extension bellows drawn out to the limit and the six-inch focal-length Zeiss Tessar lens in place, records small objects at a little less than full size.

(2) With a Proxar wide-angle lens slipped on over the Tessar,

the camera can be brought closer to the subject and the image recorded at full size.

(3) With the front element of the Tessar lens screwed out and only the rear element in use, images twice natural size are possible.

(4) And, finally, with the Tessar lens and Compur shutter removed from the camera and replaced by a one-inch focal-length Wollensack sixteen-millimetre movie-camera lens, images up to twelve diameters can be attained. The little lens is inserted in the circular opening, left by the removal of the Tessar and the Compur shutter, by means of a simple wooden mount which slips easily into place. This lens gives the most satisfactory results when used with artificial lighting.

It may be of interest to note in a little more detail how these four adjustments are used by recording the conditions under which some of the pictures shown in this volume were obtained.

In the photograph of the old-fashioned straw skep, for example, the camera was set up on a tripod and the Tessar lens alone was used. It was stopped down to f32. A one-twenty-fifth-of-a-second exposure recorded the picture on Eastman SuperXX film which was developed in D76.

For the picture of the two nectar-hunting bees on apple blossoms, the Proxar supplementary lens was slipped on over the front of the Tessar. The exposure on Eastman SuperXX film was one-fiftieth of a second at f22.

When the camera was brought even nearer for the close-up, side-view shot of the worker bee, the Proxar was removed and the front element of the Tessar unscrewed. With only the rear element employed, the image thrown on the film was approximately twice life-size. Because, under such lens conditions, the depth of focus—that is the distance between the nearest and the farthest point in the resulting picture that is sharply in focus—is very shallow, the diaphragm should always be stopped down to the smallest opening possible. With two photo-flood lamps providing the illumination, the picture was recorded on Eastman SuperXX film with an exposure of one-tenth of a second at f32.

The magnified close-ups of the faces of the worker and the drone were made with the Tessar and its attached Compur shutter removed and the whole replaced by the one-inch Wollensack lens in its circular wooden mount. With the bellows pulled out to the limit, the lens throws an image on the ground glass which has the appearance of a photomicrograph. Two photoflood lamps were placed, one six inches from the subject and the other a foot away. Even with this powerful illumination and using SuperXX film, an exposure of sixteen seconds is required when the little lens is stopped down to f16. With the lens set at f8, one wire-filled, Number O photoflash lamp provides sufficient light. When a single flash bulb is used in place of two photoflood lamps, it is well to place a sheet of white cardboard opposite the source of the illumination to reflect back some of the light and thus kill the heavy black shadow which otherwise would envelop one side of the subject. No shutter is used with this lens, the lights being turned on and off at the beginning and the end of the exposure.

In focussing such magnified pictures, I have found that modelling clay, pinched into the shape of a flexible "gooseneck," is a great aid. The insect can be placed at the end of the gooseneck and moved up or down, to this side or that, in centeing the image. Such photographs are the only ones in which it is necessary to use any except living specimens. The abnormally long exposures required make it difficult to use a live subject as the slightest movement of jaws or atennae produces a blurred image. When the image is magnified, the movement is magnified also.

Sometimes when skies are dark or a wind is lashing the plants and bushes outside, you can bring the out-of-doors to your table-top. By arranging flowers or leaves in a vase and freeing a bee near by, you can record pictures by photoflood or photoflash illumination which would be missed otherwise. One shot of the kind is the photograph of the bee obtaining pollen from fluffy pussywillows. It was made indoors on a dark and windy April day. Because of constant movement of the branches, it would have been impossible to record the shot in the open. A photoflood bulb behind and below the subject provided backlighting for the picture. The exposure on supersensitive film was one-fifth of a second at f32.

In deep shadow, out of doors, where long exposures cannot be given because of motion, a photoflash bulb will save the day. In the picture of the swarm, the clustering bees were photographed in this manner late in the afternoon. They had alighted in a wild-cherry tree where the thick foliage produced a shade so dense that a two-second exposure would have been needed even with the fastest film. By setting the camera on a tripod and using a single wire-filled flash bulb, it was possible to record the picture with detail and to stop motion at the same time.

Another outdoor picture that was made with a flash shot is the one showing the bumblebee that "came home to roost" in the hollyhock bloom. The night after the insect had been marked with a dab of white enamel, it was photographed after dark clinging in the same position, in the same flower, it had occupied the night before. The camera was focused, on a tripod, by means of the light from a hand flashlamp. Then the shutter was opened, the photoflash shot off, and the shutter closed.

Because insect pictures oftentimes have to be enlarged many times, or a small section of the original negative used for making an enlargement, films should always be developed by means of a fine-grain formula. One of the best all-round developers for this purpose is Eastman D76, purchaseable at any supply store in powder form ready for mixing. It also pays to standardize on supersensitive panchromatic films. The extra speed enables you to stop down further and get sharper detail or shoot faster to stop motion. Panchromatic film, moreover, is sensitive to all colours, including red. Other types of negative material are colour blind, seeing red as black.

Manila envelopes, or negative preservers, can be purchased cheaply and will go far toward keeping stored films free from scratches and in good condition. Frequently, when looking over your negatives after they have been sorted and put away, you see things that escaped your eye when you took the picture. This is especially true of action photographs where a number of bees are working on the comb at the same time.

One curious by-product of looking over stored negatives resulted in the series of honeycomb-pattern pictures shown in this book. I had made two shots, at different exposures, of the same piece of empty comb. Later, when I pulled the negatives, one on top of the other, from an envelope, I noticed that the overlapping images produced a striking pattern. Shifting the films this way and that, I found that different patterns formed and dissolved as the hexagonal markings changed their relative positions. By slipping the two negatives in the enlarger, I was able to record these patterns on photographic paper.

In recent years, improved and faster films, together with better aids to lighting, have increased our ability to record clear, candid-camera pictures of life in an insect commonwealth. Through the Esperanto of photography, a language that all can understand, they reveal the intimate, everyday doings of those fascinating and valuable insects, the golden dwellers of the hive.

BIBLIOGRAPHY

Beck, Bodog F., *Honey and Health*; *Bee Venom Therapy*, Appleton-Century

Bouvier, Eugene L., *The Psychic Life of Insects*, Appleton-Century

Burroughs, John, *Birds and Bees*

Cheesman, Evelyn, *Everyday Doings of Insects*, Harrap

Coleman, M. L., *Bees in the Garden and Honey in the Larder*, Doubleday, Doran

Comstock, Anna Botsford, *How to Keep Bees*, Doubleday; *Handbook of Nature Study*

Cowan, Frank, *Curious Facts in the History of Insects*, Lippincott

Dadant, Camille P., *First Lessons in Beekeeping*, American Bee Journal, Hamilton, Ill.; *The Bee Primer*, rev. ed., American Bee Journal; *Dadant System of Beekeeping*, rev. ed., American Bee Journal

Douglass, Benjamin W., *Every Step in Beekeeping*

Edwardes, Tickner, *Lore of the Honeybee*, rev. ed., Methuen; *Beekeeping for All*, Methuen

Evrard, Eugene, *The Mystery of the Hive*

Fabre, Jean Henri, *Bramble-Bees and Others*; *The Mason Bees*

Francon, J, *Mind of the Bees*, Methuen

Frey, N., *Apis the Hive Bee*, Lippincott

Gilman, A., *Practical Bee Breeding*, Putnam

Hingston, R. W. G., *Instinct and Intelligence*, Edward Arnold

Howard, Leland O., *The Insect Book*, Doubleday, Doran

Huber, François, *New Observations on the Natural History of Bees*, Root, Medina, O.

Imms, A. D., *Social Behaviour in Insects*, Methuen

Kenly, Julie C., *Cities of Wax*, Appleton-Century

Langstroth, Lorenzo L., *Langstroth on the Hive and Honey Bee*, 22nd ed., American Bee Journal

Lovell, John H., *The Flower and the Bee*, Scribner's; *Honey Plants of North America*, Root

Lubbock, John, *Ants, Bees and Wasps*

Lutz, Frank E., *Fieldbook of Insects*, Putnam

Lyon, Everett D., *How to Keep Bees for Profit*, Macmillan

Mace, H., *Book about Bees*, Hutchinson; *Adventures among Bees*, Hutchinson

Maeterlinck, Maurice, *The Life of the Bee*, Allen & Unwin; *The Children's Life of the Bee*, Allen & Unwin; *News of Spring and Other Nature Studies*, Allen & Unwin

Mason, Francis (editor), *Creation by Evolution*, Duckworth

Miller, Charles C., *A Thousand Answers to Beekeeping Questions*, American Bee Journal

Morley, Margaret W., *The Bee People*; *The Honey Makers*

Pellett, Frank C., *Beginner's Bee Book*, Lippincott; *American Honey Plants*, American Bee Journal; *Romance of the Hive*

Phillips, E. F., *Beekeeping*, rev. ed., Macmillan

Phillips, M., *Honeybees and Fairy Dust*, Harrap

Plath, Otto Emil, *Bumblebees and Their Ways*, Macmillan

Ransome, Hilda M., *The Sacred Bee*, Allen & Unwin

Réaumur, René A. F., *Natural History of the Bees*, Root

Rendl, Georg, *Way of a Bee*, Longmans

Root, A. I., and E. R., *The ABC and XYZ of Bee Culture*, Root

Root, L. C., *Mysteries of Bee Keeping*

Sharp, Dallas Lore, *The Spirit of the Hive*, Harpers

Shipley, Arthur Everett, *Studies in Insect Life*

Sladen, F. W. L., *The Humble-Bee*, Macmillan

Smithsonian Institution, Annual Report of the, 1938, Smithsonian Institution, Washington, D.C.

Snodgrass, R. E., *The Anatomy and Physiology of the Honeybee*, McGraw-Hill

Step, Edward, *Marvels of Insect Life*

Stewart, Charles David, *Fellow Creatures*

Sturges, Arthur Manning, *Practical Beekeeping*, Cassel

Thomson, J. Arthur (editor), *The Outline of Science*, Putnam

Waterman, Charles E., *Apiatia*, Root

Wells, H. G., *The Science of Life*, Cassel

Wheeler, William Morton, *The Social Insects*, Kegan, Paul; *Social Life among the Insects*, Constable

Williams, Canning, *The Story of the Hive*, Macmillan

INDEX

Alfred University, 95
Amber, 21, 22
Ant, Argentine, 68
  Jamaican, 30
Antenna, of honeybee, 40
Ants, Bees and Wasps, 135
Ants, invading hives, 67, 68
Aphides, 110
Araña Cave, 19
Assimilation, of food by bees, 46

Beck, B. F., 71, 136, 137
Bee mantis, 73
Bees, kinds of, 22
  prehistoric, 22
Beliefs, about bees, 117, 118, 119, 120,
    121, 122, 123, 124, 125, 126, 127,
    128, 129, 130
Blood, of bee, 46
  sugar content of, 46
Blue tit, 42
Bombus affinis, 27
Books, about bees, 131, 132, 133, 134,
    135, 136, 137, 138, 139
Book of Mormon, The, 117
Boswell, James, 67
Brain, of bee, 43
Bramble-Bees and Others, 136
Braula coeca, 69
Breathing, of honeybee, 45, 46
Burnens, François, 92, 98, 134
Bumblebee, 27, 28, 29, 30, 32

Carder bee, 23
Carpenter bee, 23
Catkins, alder, 38
Cell, as standard of measure, 65
  odd shaped, 65
  for storing pollen, 103
  queen, 79
  uses of, 65
Chadwick, E. A., 45

Chalicodoma muraria, 25
Cheshire, F. R., 96
Childric, I, 119
Chitin, 39
Chorion, 102
Cleanliness, of honeybees, 37, 113
Cleansing flights, 37
Clustering, in swarm, 82, 83
Cocoon, of larva, 105
Colour sense, 47, 52, 53, 54
Comstock, A. B., 136
Communication, in bees, 54, 55, 56, 57, 58
Cowan, Frank, 122, 136
Crab spider, 41
Cuckoo bees, 23
Cuculus indicator, 129
Curious Facts in the History of Insects, 122,
    136
Cyclamen, 56

Dance, of honeybees, 55
Death's-head Sphinx moth, 70
Demoll, R., 45
Deseret, 118
Desert, flowers in, 52
Distance flown by bees, 50
Dragonflies, 72
Drones, death of in mating, 94
   life of, 91
   Massacre of, 141, 142, 143, 144, 145
Duties, of young bees, 106, 107, 108

Eating bees, 75, 125
Edgerton, R. E., 54
Eggs, number laid, 96, 97
  of queen, 96, 97, 98, 101, 102
  of workers, 97, 98
Emergence, of young bees, 105
Enemies of the honeybee, 67, 68, 69, 71,
    72, 73, 74, 75, 76, 77
"Eskimo bees," 29
Eyes, of honeybee, 41, 42

Fabre, J. H., 24, 25, 26, 131, 135, 136
Florissant, 22
Flowers, number visited by bees, 50
Fossil, bees, 22
  insects, number of, 22
Frames, movable, 76
Frisch, K. von, 52, 53, 55, 56, 57, 58, 114, 138

Galleria mellonella, 69
Georgics, 128, 133
Glands, controlling activity, 108
Guards, at entrance of burrow, 26
  of stingless bees, 30

Hair, as pollinizing aid, 44
Halictidae, 26, 27
Halicatoides novae-anglae, 23, 24
Hearing, of honeybees, 42
Heating, of hive, 35, 36, 37
Hexagonal form of cells, 64, 65
Hibernation, of bumblebee queen, 28
Hingston, R. W. G., 25
Homing instinct, 42
Honey, colour of, 59, 60
  composition of, 59, 60
  food value of, 60
  how produced, 59
  mysteries of, 60
  specific gravity of, 60
  used by colony in year, 145
  value of, 20
Honeycomb, cells of, 64
  how made, 61, 62, 63, 64
  cell size, 64, 65
Honey flow, 48, 49
"Honey mines," 129
Honeysuckle, 51
Howard, Leland O., 138
Huber, François, 52, 81, 86, 88, 89, 92, 94, 98, 133, 134, 135
Hyaelus, 22, 23, 27
Hymenoptera, 21, 27, 33

Imms, A. D., 135
Innisfree, Isle of, 19
Insects, number of, 20
Instinct and Intelligence, 25

Jaws, of honeybee, 42

Johnson, Samuel, 67
Jones, D. A., 95

Kenley, Julie C., 136
Kingbird, 72
Koran, The, 117

Lancet, of sting, 76
Langstroth, L. L., 76
Larva, of honeybee, 102, 103
  increase in weight of, 103
  meals eaten by, 102
Laws of hive, 110, 111, 112, 113, 114, 115, 116
Leaf-Cutting bees, 23, 25
Legs, how used, 43
  tool kit formed by, 43, 44
Life of the Bee, The, 42, 131, 132
Lineburg, Bruce, 102
Livingstone, David, 129
Lizards, 71
Load carried by bee, 50
Loeb, Jaques, 49
Longevity, of honeybees, 49
Lubbock, John, 52, 133, 135
Lutz, F. E., 41, 51, 138

Maeterlinck, Maurice, 42, 84, 131, 132
Marey, E. J., 44, 45
Mason bees, 23, 24, 26
Mason Bees, The, 136
Massacre, of drones, 141, 142, 143, 144
Mating flight, 90, 91, 92, 93, 94, 95, 96, 97, 98, 99
McIndoo, N. E., 40
Mead, 127
Mediterranean flour moth, 71
Megachile pluto, 30
Merops apiaster, 75
Mormons, 82
Morley, M. W., 136
Motion pictures, of bees, 45
Mouse, in hive, 74
Munich Botanical Gardens, 52

Natural History of the Bees, 134
Natural History of Selborne, 75
Nest, bumblebee, 28, 29, 30
New Observations on the Natural History of Bees, 134

Observation hive, 17, 35, 44
Origin, of honeybee, 127
Odour, of honeybees, 40
Oil beetle, European, 68
Osmia bicolour, 25
Osmia fossoria, 25

Phillips, E. F., 83, 132, 137
Phlox, 56
Photography of bees, 147, 148, 149, 150, 151, 152, 153
Pickerel weed, 24
Plath, O. E., 138
Play flights, 41, 42, 107
Pliny the Elder, 52, 119, 122, 133
Pollen, use of, 38
"Pollen combs," 44
Pollination, value of, 51
Population of hive, 32
Portrait of the Honey Fly, The, 132
Praying mantis, 73, 74
Price, of honey in Egypt, 19
Propolis, 61, 70
Pussywillows, 38

Queen, bumblebee, 27, 28, 29, 30, 32
    honeybee, 32, 72, 76, 82, 83, 84, 85, 86, 87, 88, 90, 91, 92, 93, 94, 95, 96, 97, 98, 99, 101, 102, 103, 104, 109, 113, 114, 144

Ransome, Hilda M., 118, 136
Réaumur, René, A. F. de, 52, 65, 91, 133
Rig-Veda, 117
Robber fly, 72, 73
Root, E. R., 51, 137
Root, A. I., 137
Rösch, G. A., 108, 114
Rousseau, J. J., 47
Royal court, 101
Royal jelly, 32, 85, 86, 88, 97

Sacred Bee, The, 118, 136
Scent signals, at the hive, 84
    while swarming, 83
Sense plates, 40
Size, of heating cluster, 36
Skeleton, of honeybee, 39
Skunks, 71

Skunk cabbage, 37
Smell, organs of, 39, 40
    sense of in bees, 53
Snail-shell nests, 23, 25
Snodgrass, R. E., 138
Solitary bees, number of, 23
Souvenirs Entomologiques, 136
Spiders, 71
Spirit of the hive, 80, 113, 114, 116
Sting, of honeybee, 46, 47
Stingless bees, 28, 30, 31, 32
Swammerdam, Jan, 90, 128
Swarm, of honeybees, 79, 80, 81, 82, 83, 84
    prognosticating by, 124
    tone, 80
Sugar, in honeybee blood, 46

Talmud, The, 123
Telling the Bees, 120
Temperature, of brood comb, 104
    effect on cluster, 37
    effect on muscles, 37
    of individual bees, 35
    use in comb building, 61
Termite nests, 31
Thomson, J. A., 57, 136
Thorax, of honeybee, 43
Toads, 71
Tongue, of honeybee, 42
Trigona duckei, 30

Ultra-Violet light, 41
U. S. Department of Agriculture, 40, 50, 83, 95, 102

Variations in behaviour, 18, 50, 51
Venom, of sting, 77
    medicinal uses of, 77, 78
Virgil, 122, 128, 133

Warfare, use of bees in, 129
Watson, L. R., 95
Wax, of honeybee, 28, 61, 62, 63, 64, 65
    moth, 69
    plates, 46
    shears, 44
    worm, 70

Weight, of honeybee, 39
Wheeler, W. M., 30, 138
White, Gilbert, 23, 75
Whittier, J. G., 120
Wildman, Daniel, 128
Wings, of honeybee, 44, 45

Wisdom and Destiny, 131

Yeats, W. B., 19
Yellow Jackets, 74

Zeus, 118